THE UNITED STATES COOKBOOK

FABULOUS FOODS AND FASCINATING FACTS FROM ALL 50 STATES

Joan D'Amico
Karen Eich Drummond, Ed.D., R.D.

Illustrations by Jeff Cline
and Tina Cash-Walsh

John Wiley & Sons, Inc.
New York • Chichester • Weinheim • Brisbane • Singapore • Toronto

With gratitude and pride, to our country's greatest resource: its children.

Published by John Wiley & Sons, Inc.
Published simultaneously in Canada

Maps and humorous illustrations © 2000 by Jeff Cline
Illustrations of cooking utensils © 1995 by Tina Cash-Walsh

Design and production by Navta Associates, Inc.

The publisher and the author have made every reasonable effort to ensure that the experiments and activities in this book are safe when conducted as instructed but assume no responsibility for any damage caused or sustained while performing the experiments or activities in the book. Parents, guardians, and/or teachers should supervise young readers who undertake the experiments and activities in this book.

Library of Congress Cataloging-in-Publication Data

D'Amico, Joan
    The United States cookbook : fabulous foods and fascinating facts from all 50 states / Joan D'Amico and Karen Eich Drummond.
      p.   cm.
    Includes index.
    Summary: Provides information about the fifty states along with a recipe native to each of them, such as Boston baked beans from Massachusetts, crab cakes from Maryland, Key lime pie from Florida, corn dogs from Iowa, and taco soup from New Mexico.
    ISBN 0-471-35839-8 (pbk. : alk. paper)
    1. Cookery, American.   2. Cookery—United States. [1. Cookery, American.] I. Drummond, Karen Eich.   II. Title.
TX715.D18194   2000
641.5973—dc21   99-39548

Printed in the United States of America

10 9 8 7 6 5 4

CONTENTS

ABOUT THIS BOOK 1

DISCOVERING THE KITCHEN 3

Tools of the Trade 4

Cooking Skills   Cutting 7

Measuring 8

Mixing 8

Stovetop Cooking 9

Cracking and Separating Eggs 9

Safety Rules   Around the Stove and Oven 11

Using Any Appliance 12

Using a Microwave Oven 12

Using a Knife 13

Cleaning Up 13

PART 1   NEW ENGLAND 15

Chapter 1   **Connecticut**—The Constitution State 16

Election Day Cake 17

Chapter 2   **Maine**—The Pine Tree State 19

Blueberry Cornbread 20

Chapter 3   **Massachusetts**—The Bay State 22

Boston Baked Beans 23

Chapter 4   **New Hampshire**—The Granite State 25

Raspberry and Apple Cobbler 26

Chapter 5   **Rhode Island**—The Ocean State 28

Coffee Milkshakes 29

Chapter 6   **Vermont**—The Green Mountain State 31

Banana Berry Pancakes with Real Maple Syrup 32

PART 2 THE MIDDLE ATLANTIC 35

    Chapter 7   **Delaware**—The First State.................................36
                      Classic Gingerbread Squares 37
    Chapter 8   **Maryland**—The Old Line State 39
                      Maryland Baked Crab Cakes 40
    Chapter 9   **New Jersey**—The Garden State.........................42
                      Italian Submarine Sandwiches 43
    Chapter 10   **New York**—The Empire State 45
                      Waldorf Salad 46
    Chapter 11   **Pennsylvania**—The Keystone State.....................48
                      Philadelphia Soft Pretzels..49

PART 3 THE SOUTH 51

    Chapter 12   **Alabama**—The Heart of Dixie...........................52
                      Sweet Potato Biscuits...53
    Chapter 13   **Arkansas**—The Land of Opportunity 55
                      Chocolate Rice Pudding 56
    Chapter 14   **Florida**—The Sunshine State................................58
                      Key Lime Pie 59
    Chapter 15   **Georgia**—The Peach State 61
                      Peanutty Peanut Butter and Banana Bread.................62
    Chapter 16   **Kentucky**—The Bluegrass State.............................64
                      Kentucky Burgoo 65
    Chapter 17   **Louisiana**—The Pelican State...........................67
                      New Orleans *Pain Perdu* 68
    Chapter 18   **Mississippi**—The Magnolia State 70
                      Mississippi Mud Pie 71
    Chapter 19   **North Carolina**—The Tar Heel State.....................73
                      North Carolina BBQ 74
    Chapter 20   **South Carolina**—The Palmetto State 76
                      Peach Roll 77
    Chapter 21   **Tennessee**—The Volunteer State 79
                      German Potato Salad...80

Chapter 22   **Virginia**—The Old Dominion 82
             Virginia Ham with Cherry Sauce 83
Chapter 23   **West Virginia**—The Mountain State....................85
             Golden Delicious Apple Pie...................................86

PART 4

THE MIDWEST 89

Chapter 24   **Illinois**—The Prairie State 90
             Deep-Dish Pizza 91
Chapter 25   **Indiana**—The Hoosier State 93
             Bread Pudding...94
Chapter 26   **Iowa**—The Hawkeye State................................96
             Corn Dogs 97
Chapter 27   **Kansas**—Midway U.S.A. 99
             Grilled Swiss Cheeseburger with Sliced Mushrooms ..100
Chapter 28   **Michigan**—The Wolverine State 102
             Ice Cream with Cherry Sauce in a Tortilla Shell.........103
Chapter 29   **Minnesota**—The Land of 10,000 Lakes 105
             Swedish Meatballs 106
Chapter 30   **Missouri**—The Show Me State...........................108
             Black Walnut Quickbread 109
Chapter 31   **Nebraska**—The Cornhusker State.......................111
             Reuben Sandwich..112
Chapter 32   **North Dakota**—The Flickertail State....................114
             Macaroni and Cheese 115
Chapter 33   **Ohio**—The Buckeye State 117
             Cincinnati Chili over Pasta 118
Chapter 34   **South Dakota**—The Land of Infinite Variety 120
             Cornmeal Mush with Molasses 121
Chapter 35   **Wisconsin**—America's Dairyland........................123
             Wisconsin Cheddar Dill Puffs...............................124

PART 5

THE SOUTHWEST 127

Chapter 36   **Arizona**—The Grand Canyon State 128
             Cheese Quesadilla with Vegetables.......................129

Chapter 37 **New Mexico**—The Land of Enchantment..............131
Taco Soup...132
Chapter 38 **Oklahoma**—The Sooner State..........................134
Peanut Blondie Bars 135
Chapter 39 **Texas**—The Lone Star State 137
Spicy Barbecue Sauce 138

PART
6 THE ROCKY MOUNTAINS 141
Chapter 40 **Colorado**—The Centennial State.....................142
Denver Sandwich 143
Chapter 41 **Idaho**—The Gem State 145
Baked Sliced Potatoes 146
Chapter 42 **Montana**—Big Sky Country..........................148
Cheyenne Batter Bread 149
Chapter 43 **Nevada**—The Sagebrush State........................151
Onion Rings 152
Chapter 44 **Utah**—The Beehive State.............................154
Mallo-Mallo Fudge Squares............................155
Chapter 45 **Wyoming**—The Cowboy State 157
Rancher's Beef Pot Pies 158

PART
7 THE PACIFIC STATES 161
Chapter 46 **Alaska**—The Last Frontier.............................162
Baked Salmon 163
Chapter 47 **California**—The Golden State..........................165
Classic Caesar Salad.....................................166
Chapter 48 **Hawaii**—The Aloha State 168
Pineapple Chicken Kabobs 169
Chapter 49 **Oregon**—The Beaver State 171
Cranberry Cookie Bars..................................172
Chapter 50 **Washington**—The Evergreen State....................174
Baked Apples 175

INDEX 177

ABOUT THIS BOOK

If cooking and eating your way across the United States sounds like fun, this is the book for you. It's a lively and exciting trip, starting way up in the northeastern United States and traveling across to the Pacific Ocean. Along the way, you will learn about the history and foods of each state.

You'll make delicious recipes like Italian Submarine Sandwiches, Election Day Cake, Philadelphia Soft Pretzels, and Corn Dogs. Some recipes are state traditions, like Kentucky Burgoo. Some were brought to the United States by immigrants from faraway lands, and others were introduced to early settlers by Native Americans. Each state produces a variety of native and introduced food products and some recipes feature these foods, such as Washington apples.

Before you start this book, be sure to read the "Discovering the Kitchen" section that starts on page 3. It covers the basics on kitchen safety, utensils, cooking terms, and measuring. Each recipe lists how much time you will need to make it, the kitchen tools you'll need, and the number of servings it makes.

From the first state, Delaware, to the fiftieth state, Hawaii, we hope you appreciate the diversity and the cooking traditions of the people who have made American cooking as exciting as it is today. Enjoy your trip and don't forget to send a postcard.

Joan D'Amico, M.A., LDT-C.　　Karen Eich Drummond, Ed.D., R.D.
Wayne, New Jersey　　　　　　　　　　Yardley, Pennsylvania

DISCOVERING THE KITCHEN

Tools of the Trade

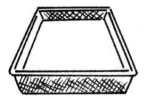

baking pan

biscuit cutter

cookie
sheet

electric
blender

electric
mixer

colander

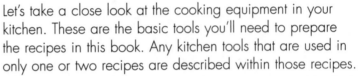
cutting board

Let's take a close look at the cooking equipment in your kitchen. These are the basic tools you'll need to prepare the recipes in this book. Any kitchen tools that are used in only one or two recipes are described within those recipes.

baking pan   A square or rectangular pan used for baking and cooking foods in the oven. The most common sizes are 9 × 13-inch and 8-inch square.

biscuit cutter   A round outline, usually made from metal, used to cut biscuits from dough.

colander   A large perforated bowl used for rinsing food and draining pasta or other foods.

cookie sheet   A large rectangular pan with no sides or with half-inch sides, used for baking cookies and other foods.

cutting board   Made from wood or plastic, cutting boards provide a surface on which to cut foods.

egg separator   A small, shallow metal cup with slots used to separate the egg whites from the yolk. The yolk sits in the middle while the whites drop through the slots into a bowl.

electric blender   A glass or plastic cylinder with a rotating blade at the bottom. A small motor in the base turns the blade. The blender has different speeds and is used for mixing, blending, grinding, and pureeing.

electric mixer   Two beaters that rotate to mix ingredients together. Used for mashed potatoes, cake batters, and other mixing jobs.

grater   A metal surface with sharp-edged holes used for shredding and grating foods such as vegetables and cheese.

knives:

- **paring knife**   A knife with a small pointed blade used for trimming and paring vegetables and fruits and other cutting jobs that don't require a larger knife. (Most recipes in this book call for a knife. You will find the paring knife works well in most situations.)

- **peeler**   A handheld tool that removes the peel from fruits and vegetables.

- **sandwich spreader**   A knife with a dull blade that is designed to spread fillings on bread.

- **table knife**   A knife used as a utensil at the table.

layer cake pans   Round metal pans used to bake layers of a cake.

measuring cups   Cups with measurements (½ cup, ⅓ cup, etc.) on the side, bottom, or handle. Measuring cups that have spouts are used for liquid ingredients. Measuring cups without spouts are used for dry ingredients such as flour.

measuring spoons   Used for measuring small amounts of foods such as spices. They come in a set of 1 tablespoon, 1 teaspoon, ½ teaspoon, and ¼ teaspoon.

microwave dish   A dish that can safely be used in the microwave oven. The best microwave dishes say "microwave safe" on the label. Don't use metal pans, aluminum foil, plastic foam containers, brown paper bags, plastic wrap, or margarine tubs in the microwave.

mixing bowls   Round-bottomed bowls used for mixing and whipping all kinds of foods. Depending on the amount of ingredients, a large, medium, or small bowl may be used.

muffin tins   Metal or glass pans with small, round cups used for baking muffins and cupcakes.

grater

paring knife

sandwich spreader

layer cake pan

measuring cup

measuring spoons

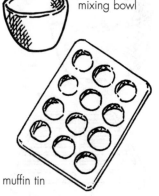

mixing bowl

muffin tin

frying pan

saucepan

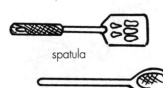

pastry
blender

rolling pin

rubber spatula

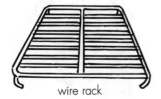

spatula

wooden spoon

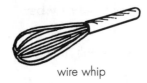

tube pan

wire rack

pans:

- **frying pan** (also called a sauté pan)   Used for cooking foods, such as hamburgers or onions, in hot fat.

- **saucepan** (also called a pot)   Used for general stovetop cooking, such as boiling pasta or simmering a sauce.

pastry blender   A group of stiff wires attached to both ends of a handle. It is used, with a rocking motion, to blend butter or margarine into flour and other dry ingredients to make a dough.

rolling pin   A wooden or plastic roller used to flatten items such as pie crust and biscuit dough.

rubber spatula   A flat, flexible rubber or plastic tip on a long handle. It is used to scrape bowls, pots, and pans and for **folding** (a gentle over-and-under motion) ingredients into whipped cream or other whipped batter.

spatula   A flat metal or plastic tool used for lifting and turning meats, eggs, and other foods.

spoons:

- **teaspoon**   A spoon used for measuring. Also the name for the spoon normally used as a utensil at the table.

- **wooden spoon**   Used for mixing ingredients together and stirring.

tube pan   A metal cake pan with a center tube used for making angel food cakes, bundt cakes, and special breads.

wire rack   Used for cooling baked goods.

wire whip   Used especially for whipping egg whites and cream.

wire whip

COOKING SKILLS

Chefs need to master cutting and measuring skills and the basics of mixing and stovetop cooking. Here are the skills you will be practicing as you try the recipes in this book.

CUTTING

Foods are cut before cooking so that they will look good and cook evenly. Place the food to be cut on a cutting board and use a knife that is a comfortable size for your hand. To hold the knife, place your hand on top of the handle and fit your fingers around the handle. The grip should be secure but relaxed. In your other hand, hold the item being cut. Keep your fingertips curled under to protect them from cuts. (See the "Safety Rules" section on page 11 for more on how to cut safely.)

Here are some commonly used cutting terms you'll need to know:

chop   To cut into irregularly shaped pieces.

dice   To cut into cubes of the same size.

mince   To chop very fine.

slice   To cut into uniform slices.

Grating and shredding are also examples of cutting:

grate   To rub a food across a grater's tiny punched holes to produce small or fine pieces of food. Hard cheeses and some vegetables are grated.

shred   To rub a food across a surface with medium to large holes or slits. Shredded foods look like strips. The cheese used for making pizza is always shredded.

chopped

diced

minced

sliced

grate

shred

Equivalents

1 tablespoon = 3 teaspoons
1 cup = 16 tablespoons
1 cup = 8 fluid ounces
1 quart = 2 pints
1 quart = 4 cups
1 quart = 32 fluid ounces
1 gallon = 4 quarts
1 stick butter or margarine
= ½ cup = 8 tablespoons

MEASURING

Ingredients can be measured in three different ways: by counting (six apples), by measuring volume (½ cup of applesauce), or by measuring weight (a pound of apples).

To measure the volume of a liquid, always place the measuring cup on a flat surface and check that the liquid goes up to the proper line on the measuring cup while you are looking directly at it at eye level.

To measure the volume of a dry ingredient, such as flour, spoon it into the measuring cup and level it off with a table knife. Do not pack the cup with the dry ingredient—that is, don't press down on it to make room for more—unless the recipe says to.

liquid
measurement

dry
measurement

beat

fold

whip

MIXING

There are all kinds of ways to mix! Here are definitions of the most common types.

beat　To move a utensil back and forth to blend ingredients together.

cream　To mix a solid fat (usually margarine or butter) and sugar by pressing them against a bowl with the back of a spoon until they look creamy.

fold　To move a utensil with a gentle over-and-under motion.

mix　To combine ingredients so that they are all evenly distributed.

whip　To beat rapidly using a circular motion, usually with a whip, to incorporate air into the mixture (such as in making whipped cream).

whisk　To beat ingredients together lightly with a wire whip until they are well blended.

STOVETOP COOKING

There are different ways to cook on your stove. Here are descriptions of cooking methods you will be practicing as you try the recipes in this book. Because it is easy to get burned while cooking on the stove, see the "Safety Rules" section on page 11.

boil   To heat a liquid to its boiling point, or to cook in a boiling liquid. Water boils at 212°F. You can tell it is boiling when you see lots of large bubbles popping to the surface. When a liquid boils, it is turning into steam (the gaseous state of water). Water can't get any hotter than 212°F; it can only make steam faster. Boiling is most often used for cooking pasta.

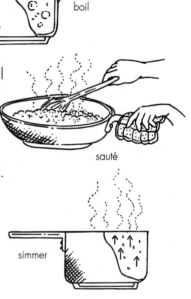

boil

sauté

pan-fry   To cook in a pan over moderate heat in a small amount of fat. Hamburgers are an example of a food that can be pan-fried.

sauté   To cook quickly in a pan over medium-high heat in a small amount of fat. Vegetables, especially onions, are often sautéed in oil to bring out their flavor and brown them.

simmer   To heat a liquid to just below its boiling point, or to cook in a simmering liquid. You can tell a liquid is simmering when it has bubbles floating slowly to the surface. Most foods cooked in liquid are simmered. Always watch simmering foods closely so that they do not boil.

simmer

steam   To cook in steam. Steam has much more heat and cooks foods more quickly than boiling water does. Steaming is an excellent method for cooking most vegetables.

CRACKING AND SEPARATING EGGS

It is best to crack an egg into a clear glass cup (such as a measuring cup) before adding it to the other ingredients. That way, if the egg smells bad or has a red spot, you can throw it out before the egg goes in with the other ingredients. An egg with a red spot is safe to eat but is

usually thrown out because of its appearance. You should also remove any pieces of eggshell from the egg before adding the egg to the other ingredients.

Sometimes you will need to separate the egg yolk from the egg white for a recipe. To do this, crack the egg over an egg separator and a bowl. Make sure you get the yolk in the middle. The whites will drain out into the bowl. If you don't have an egg separator, you can separate an egg by cracking it over a bowl, keeping the yolk in one half of the shell. Carefully pass the egg yolk from one half of the shell to the other without letting it break until the white has fallen into the bowl.

SAFETY RULES

The kitchen can be a safe, or a very dangerous, part of your home. What's dangerous in your kitchen? Sharp knives, boiling water, and hot oil are a few things. Always check with an adult before trying any of the recipes. Talk to him or her about what you are allowed to do by yourself and when you need an adult's assistance. And always follow these safety guidelines.

AROUND THE STOVE AND OVEN

- Get an adult's permission before you use a stove or oven.
- Don't wear long, baggy shirts or sweaters when cooking. They could catch fire.
- Never turn your back on a frying pan that contains oil.
- Never fry with oil at a high temperature.
- Don't spray a pan with vegetable oil cooking spray over the stove or near heat. Oil will burn at high temperatures, so spray the pan over the sink.
- If a fire starts in a pan on the stove, you can smother it by covering it with the pan lid or pouring baking soda on it. Never use water to put out a fire in a pan with oil—it only makes a fire worse.
- Always use pot holders or wear oven mitts when using the oven or handling something that is hot. Make sure your pot holders are not wet. Wet pot holders transmit the heat from the hot item you are holding directly to your skin.
- Don't overfill pans with boiling or simmering liquids.
- Open pan lids away from you to let steam escape safely.

- Keep pan handles turned away from the edge of the stove. Knocking against them can splatter hot food.
- Stir foods with long-handled spoons.
- Keep pets and small children away from hot stoves and ovens during cooking. (Try to keep them out of the kitchen altogether.)

USING ANY APPLIANCE

- Use an appliance only if you know exactly how to operate it and you have permission from an adult.
- Never operate an appliance that is near the sink or sitting in water.
- Don't use frayed electrical cords or damaged plugs and outlets. Tell an adult.

USING A MICROWAVE OVEN

- Use only microwave-safe cookware, paper towels, paper plates, or paper cups.
- Use pot holders or oven mitts to remove items.
- If a dish is covered, make sure there is some opening through which steam can escape during cooking.
- When taking foods out of the microwave, you must open the container so that steam escapes *away* from your hands and face.
- Prick foods like potatoes and hot dogs with a fork before putting them into the microwave.
- Never try to cook a whole egg in the microwave—it will burst!

USING A KNIFE

- Get an adult's permission before using any knife.

- Always pick up a knife by its handle.

- Pay attention to what you're doing!

- Cut away from the body and away from anyone near you.

- Use a sliding, back-and-forth motion when slicing foods with a knife.

- Don't leave a knife near the edge of a table. It can be easily knocked off, or a small child may touch it.

- Don't try to catch a falling knife.

- Don't use knives to cut string, to open cans or bottles, or as a screwdriver.

- Don't put a knife into a sink full of water. Instead, put it on the drainboard, to avoid cutting yourself.

CLEANING UP

Whenever you use a knife and cutting board to cut meat, poultry, or seafood, be sure to wash them thoroughly before using them again. These foods contain germs that can be harmful, and you don't want the germs to get onto foods that won't be cooked, such as vegetables for salads.

NEW ENGLAND

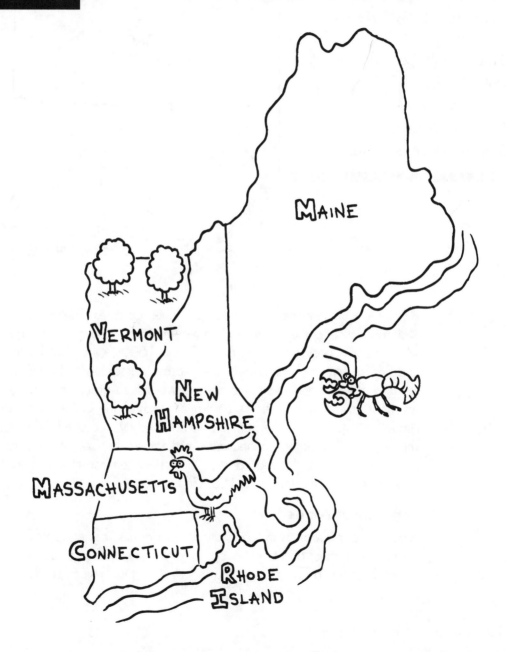

CHAPTER 1

ONNECTICUT
The Constitution State

Capital: Hartford

Other Major Cities: New Haven, Norwich

State Animal: Sperm Whale

State Bird: Robin

State Insect: Praying Mantis

State Tree: White Oak

State Flower: Mountain Laurel

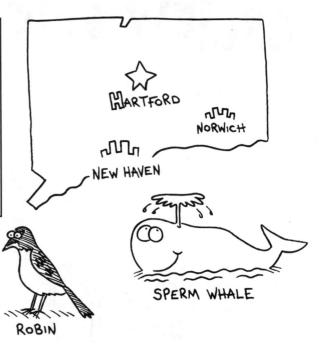

Connecticut was one of the original thirteen colonies. The name Connecticut comes from the Native American word *quinnehtukqet,* which means "beside the long river." By the 1600s, when Dutch settlers and English settlers unhappy with the nearby Massachusetts Bay Colony first moved into Connecticut, there were over fifteen groups of Native Americans living in the area. Their names, such as the Quinnipiac and Pequot, are recalled in the names of towns and rivers around the state. The third smallest state, Connecticut is nicknamed the Constitution State. Its state constitution was regarded as the first written constitution, and it also served as a model for the U.S. Constitution.

Connecticut Foods

Important farm products in Connecticut include milk, eggs, apples, pears, mushrooms, and beef. Because it has an extensive coastline, Connecticut has a booming fishing industry. Clams, oysters, scallops, and flounder are big catches.

···· Election Day Cake ····

In colonial days, election days meant sermons, parades, and feasting. One of the time-honored foods was a cake full of raisins and citron, the candied rind from a citrus fruit such as a lemon. In our updated version of this recipe, we have substituted chocolate chips for the citron.

Ingredients

1 tablespoon vegetable shortening

½ cup milk

½ cup warm water

2 packages active dry yeast

1½ cups sifted whole wheat flour

2 cups sifted all-purpose flour

1 teaspoon salt

2 teaspoons cinnamon

½ teaspoon mace

½ teaspoon ground nutmeg

½ teaspoon ground cloves

½ cup margarine

¾ cup sugar

3 large eggs, well beaten

1 cup chopped dried fruit pieces

½ cup raisins

½ cup chocolate chips

¼ cup slivered almonds

Time
70 minutes to prepare
plus
2 hours rising time
plus
50 to 55 minutes to bake

Tools
10-inch bundt pan

small saucepan

2 large bowls

measuring cup

wooden spoon

plastic wrap

medium bowl

oven mitts

Makes
12 servings

Steps

1. Grease the bundt pan with the vegetable shortening.

2. In the small saucepan, heat the milk until it almost reaches a simmer. Stop when you see some steam coming from the pan. Pour the milk into a large bowl.

3. Put the warm water into the measuring cup and sprinkle in the yeast. Do not stir. Let the yeast stand for about 5 minutes or until it gets foamy. Add the yeast mixture to the milk.

4. Add the whole wheat flour to the milk mixture and beat with the wooden spoon until smooth. Cover the bowl with plastic wrap and let the batter rise in a warm place for 1 hour until it is bubbly.

5. In the medium bowl, combine the all-purpose flour, salt, cinnamon, mace, nutmeg, and cloves. Set aside.

6. In the other large bowl, beat the margarine and sugar together until fluffy. Add the eggs and mix thoroughly.

7. Stir in the milk mixture.

8. Gradually add the dry ingredients, beating with the wooden spoon until smooth and well blended. The batter will be thick.

9. Stir in the dried fruit pieces, raisins, chocolate chips, and almond slivers and mix well.

10. Turn the mixture into the bundt pan. Cover loosely with plastic wrap and let rise for about 2 hours in a warm place without any drafts. (The inside of the microwave can be a good spot.) The cake is ready to be baked when the dough almost reaches the top of the bundt pan. When you think the dough is nearly ready, preheat the oven to 350°F.

11. Bake for 50 to 55 minutes. Allow the cake to cool for 20 minutes before taking it out of the pan. Cool the cake completely before serving.

Fabulous Food Festival
Lobster Weekend
Mystic (May)

FUN FOOD FACTS

- The French are credited with bringing to New England their tradition of chowder, a type of thick soup made with fish, seafood, and vegetables. The word *chowder* comes from the French name for a big copper pot, *chaudière*, in which the soup was prepared.

- The world's first lollipop was made in New Haven in 1908.

- The hamburger was probably first made and sold in New Haven in 1900. The owner of Louis' Lunch made hamburgers from the trimmings of steak used in steak sandwiches. He served the hamburgers on a plate with onions and home fries. When a customer was in a rush, he asked the owner to put the hamburger between two pieces of bread so he could get going. Even in 1900 there was a need for fast food!

- Domestic ducks were first raised in Connecticut after a clipper ship brought some from faraway Peking.

CHAPTER 2
MAINE
The Pine Tree State

Capital: Augusta

Other Major Cities: Bangor, Portland

State Animals: Maine Coon Cat, Moose

State Bird: Black-capped Chickadee

State Insect: Honeybee

State Tree: White Pine

State Flower: White Pinecone and Tassel

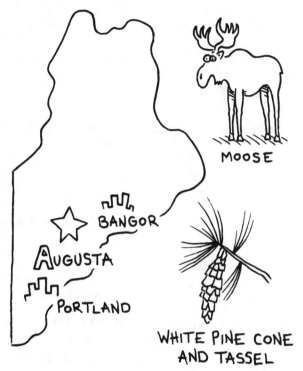

MOOSE

BANGOR

AUGUSTA

PORTLAND

WHITE PINE CONE AND TASSEL

If you want to be the first person in the United States to see the sun rise in the morning, make sure you're in Eastport, Maine, the easternmost town in the country. The origin of Maine's name is not really certain. Some say English explorers called it Maine as a shortened form for mainland. Others say it was named after an area of France called Maine. Maine was part of the colony, and then the state, of Massachusetts until 1820. At that time, Mainers voted to separate from Massachusetts and Maine was accepted as the twenty-third state. Because of its large evergreen forests, it is nicknamed the Pine Tree State.

Maine Foods

Maine is the country's number one source of blueberries and lobster. Over 90 percent of U.S. lobsters come from Maine. With its long, rocky coastline, Maine is a top fishing state. In addition to lobster, Maine provides lots of clams and other seafood. Mainers even make clamburgers out of chopped clams.

Blueberry Cornbread

Tools
paper towel

9-inch square baking pan

2 medium bowls

colander

small bowl

wooden spoon

wire whip

rubber spatula

oven mitts

Makes
6 to 8 servings

Mainers love to use blueberries in many different recipes, such as muffins, pancakes, puddings, and pies. This recipe uses blueberries to give cornbread a unique sweetness.

Ingredients

2 teaspoons vegetable shortening

1 cup all-purpose flour

1 cup yellow cornmeal

¼ cup sugar

1 tablespoon baking powder

½ teaspoon salt

1 cup blueberries

1 cup milk

¼ cup canola oil

¼ cup honey

2 large eggs, slightly beaten

Steps

1. Preheat the oven to 400°F. Use the paper towel to grease the baking pan with the shortening.

2. In a medium bowl, mix together the flour and cornmeal. Stir well to combine. Add the sugar, baking powder, and salt and stir again.

3. Wash the blueberries in the colander. Pat dry.

4. Place the blueberries in the small bowl. Add 2 tablespoons of the flour mixture and gently toss the flour and the blueberries with a wooden spoon. Set aside.

5. In the other medium bowl, whisk together the milk, oil, honey, and eggs.

6. Add the milk mixture to the dry ingredients and stir together just until the ingredients are well moistened.

7. With the rubber spatula, fold in the blueberries.

8. Pour the batter into the greased baking pan.

9. Bake for 20 to 25 minutes or until the bread is a light golden brown.

FUN FOOD FACTS

- In northernmost Maine (*brr!*) is Aroostock County. No, it is not known for roosters, but potatoes! More potatoes are grown in Aroostock County than in any other county in the United States.

- The first commercial chewing gum was invented in 1848 in Bangor, Maine. But Native Americans were really the first to chew gum. Actually they chewed the resin of the black spruce tree, supposedly as a way to fight off hunger.

- Lobster wasn't always considered a delicacy. Residents of an early Maine settlement protested vigorously against being served lobster at every meal.

Fabulous Food Festival
Clam Festival
Yarmouth
(July)

CHAPTER 3
MASSACHUSETTS
The Bay State

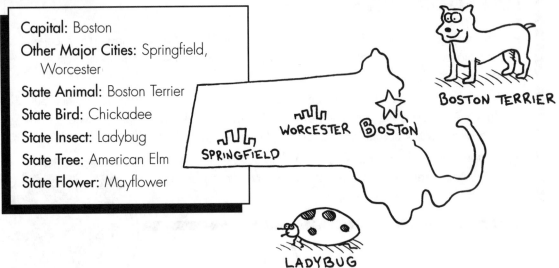

Capital: Boston

Other Major Cities: Springfield, Worcester

State Animal: Boston Terrier

State Bird: Chickadee

State Insect: Ladybug

State Tree: American Elm

State Flower: Mayflower

SPRINGFIELD

WORCESTER BOSTON

BOSTON TERRIER

LADYBUG

The Pilgrims landed at Plymouth, in what is now Massachusetts, in 1620. Knowing very little about hunting or farming in this new land, the Pilgrims might never have survived if it hadn't been for the helpful Wampanoag Indians they met. The following year with their new friends they celebrated America's first big food event: Thanksgiving. The menu included wild turkeys, ducks, geese, deer, cod, squashes, corn, beans, cranberry sauce sweetened with maple sugar, and bread.

Massachusetts was one of the original thirteen British colonies, and it was the center of much activity during the Revolutionary War. The Boston Tea Party, despite its name, wasn't actually a party. It was a protest against British taxes (which were particularly heavy on tea) that helped spark the Revolutionary War.

The state of Massachusetts was named for a Native American tribe of the same name. The name is thought to mean "near the great hill." Massachusetts is nicknamed the Bay State because of all its bays (an area where a body of water forms an indentation of the shoreline).

••••••••••••• Boston Baked Beans ••••••••••••••

Early colonists learned to make baked beans from their Native American neighbors. Native Americans flavored the beans with bear meat and maple syrup. The colonists substituted salt pork for the bear meat and molasses for the maple syrup. Baked beans on Saturday night became a Massachusetts food tradition in colonial times. The tradition started because the Puritans were not allowed to work on Sunday, so beans were cooked on Saturday and served for Sunday's dinner as well. Some women who were not so crazy about beans served them only on Sunday.

Ingredients

1 medium onion
vegetable oil cooking spray
2 16-ounce cans navy beans
1 15-ounce can pinto beans

⅓ cup ketchup
3 tablespoons brown sugar
2 tablespoons molasses
1 tablespoon spicy brown mustard

Time
20 minutes to prepare
plus
30 minutes to cook

Tools
cutting board

paring knife

large sauté pan

can opener

colander

2-quart casserole dish
with cover

oven mitts

Makes
6 servings

Steps

1. Preheat the oven to 400°F.

2. Remove the skin from the onion. On the cutting board, use the knife to cut the onion in half. Lay the onion halves cut-side down on the cutting board and chop.

3. Spray the sauté pan with vegetable oil cooking spray. Heat the sauté pan over medium heat.

4. Add the onions and sauté until soft, about 5 minutes.

5. Open the 3 cans of beans. Put the beans in the colander in the sink and rinse them under cold, running water.

6. In the casserole, stir together the onions, beans, ketchup, brown sugar, molasses, and mustard.

7. Cover and bake for 30 minutes until the mixture is bubbly.

Massachusetts Foods

Massachusetts grows more cranberries than any other state. Most cranberries are grown on Cape Cod in wet areas called bogs. Cranberries need a large supply of water nearby so growers can flood the bog to protect the plants from insects, disease, and frost. During harvesting, the bogs are also flooded. The cranberries, which have tiny air pockets inside, float to the surface, and are gathered by harvesters who wade in the water with big rakes to collect the crop. Other farm products include milk and eggs. Massachusetts is also a leader in fishing, and fishing boats bring in lots of scallops, cod, and haddock.

FUN FOOD FACTS

- Sometime in the 1930s, the innkeeper's wife at the Toll House Inn near Whitman added chocolate pieces to her drop cookie recipe. She called her cookies Toll House Cookies. Chocolate chip cookies had been made before this time, but now they became enormously popular. When the Nestlé Company found out about the recipe, they got permission to use it on the wrapper of their chocolate bars.

- The first commercial yogurt was made in 1931 in Andover. It was sold first as a health food and only found a large market after a manufacturer had the idea of adding strawberry preserves.

- In 1939, Elsie the Cow traveled from her home in Brookfield to the New York World's Fair and became famous as the symbol of the Borden Company.

Fabulous Food Festival
Cranberry Harvest Festival
Harwich
(September)

CHAPTER 4
NEW HAMPSHIRE
The Granite State

Capital: Concord
Other Major Cities: Manchester, Rochester
State Animal: White-tailed Deer
State Bird: Purple Finch
State Insect: Ladybug
State Tree: White Birch
State Flower: Purple Lilac

PURPLE LILAC

WHITE-TAILED DEER

CONCORD
ROCHESTER
MANCHESTER

New Hampshire was named by John Mason for his home county of Hampshire in England. The first inhabitants were Native Americans who traded with the early settlers and helped them farm the land. Besides farming, the settlers also fished, cut down trees for their lumber, and hunted animals for their furs. The furs were then sold or exchanged for needed goods to fur traders who sold them in England. In 1776, before the Declaration of Independence was signed, New Hampshire formed its own independent republic. Twelve years later, in 1788, New Hampshire signed the Constitution of the United States.

New Hampshire is nicknamed the Granite State because granite, a very hard type of rock, is found under most of it. Granite is used in buildings and memorials. New Hampshire granite was used to build the Library of Congress in Washington, D.C. The state motto is "Live Free or Die." General John Stark, New Hampshire's greatest hero of the Revolutionary War, said this during the colonies' fight against England.

New Hampshire Foods

You'll see plenty of cows dotting the New Hampshire landscape, and milk is the state's most important farm product. New Hampshire is also a leading producer of maple syrup (like its neighbor, Vermont). In addition, New Hampshire produces potatoes and apples.

Raspberry and Apple Cobbler

Time
20 minutes to prepare
plus
25 minutes to bake

Tools
medium bowl

wooden spoon

pastry blender

paper towels

medium saucepan

small bowl

wire whip

2-quart baking dish

small custard cup

oven mitts

Makes
8 servings

Early settlers in New Hampshire planted apple orchards. With these apples and wild raspberries, they made cobblers. A cobbler is like a fruit pie, but it has a crumb-type topping on top instead of a crust.

Ingredients

½ cup all-purpose flour

½ cup whole wheat flour

2 tablespoons sugar

1½ teaspoons baking powder

¼ cup margarine

2 cups fresh raspberries

⅓ cup sugar

2 tablespoons cornstarch

1½ tablespoons lemon juice

¼ cup water

3 cups peeled, sliced apples (about 3 medium apples)

1 large egg

¼ cup milk

1 tablespoon sugar

½ teaspoon cinnamon

¼ teaspoon ground nutmeg

¼ cup chopped walnuts

ice cream or frozen yogurt (optional)

Steps

1. Preheat the oven to 400°F.

2. In the medium bowl, mix together the flours, 2 tablespoons of the sugar, and the baking powder with the wooden spoon.

3. Cut the margarine into the mixture with the pastry blender, using a back-and-forth motion until the mixture looks like small peas. Set aside.

4. Wash the raspberries gently and place them on paper towels to dry. Set aside.

5. In the saucepan, mix together ⅓ cup of sugar and the cornstarch. Add the raspberries, lemon juice, and water. Heat on low and stir until smooth.

6. Cook the raspberry mixture until thickened and bubbly, about 5 minutes. Stir in the apples and cook for about 3 more minutes. Set the filling aside.

7. In the small bowl, whisk the egg until foamy. Add the milk.

8. Pour the milk and egg mixture all at once into the flour mixture. Stir just until the mixture is moistened.

9. Place the raspberry filling into the baking dish.

10. Using a tablespoon, put all of the flour mixture over the filling so that the filling is covered.

11. In the custard cup, mix together 1 tablespoon sugar, the cinnamon, and the nutmeg. Sprinkle the mixture over the cobbler topping. Cover with walnuts.

12. Bake for 25 minutes or until the cobbler topping is a light golden brown. Serve with ice cream or frozen yogurt if desired.

FUN FOOD FACTS

- One New Hampshire dish, Red Flannel Hash, may sound as if you'd be eating your pajamas, but it's really a tasty combination of leftover corned beef, red beets, and other vegetables.

- Five shiploads of Scotch-Irish families arrived in New Hampshire in 1719 with potatoes that they planted. Most Europeans at that time considered potatoes food for pigs, not humans. These families harvested their first crop in time to eat during their first winter. Within twenty years, potatoes had become an important crop in the colony.

Fabulous Food Festival
Mount Washington Valley Chocolate Festival
North Conway
(February)

CHAPTER 5

RHODE ISLAND
The Ocean State

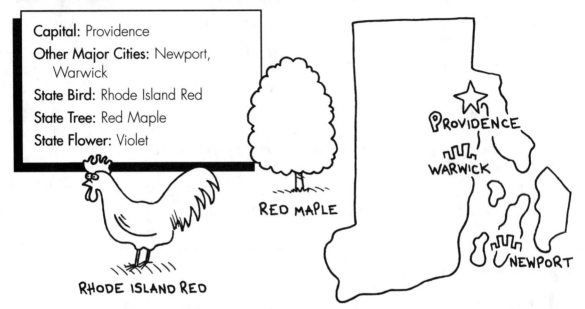

Capital: Providence
Other Major Cities: Newport, Warwick
State Bird: Rhode Island Red
State Tree: Red Maple
State Flower: Violet

RED MAPLE

RHODE ISLAND RED

PROVIDENCE

WARWICK

NEWPORT

Rhode Island is the nation's smallest state but it has the biggest official name: State of Rhode Island and Providence Plantations. In the early 1600s, Roger Williams was banished from the Massachusetts Bay Colony because of religious and political beliefs, and he founded the English settlement at Providence on Narragansett Bay. (Narragansett Bay was named after the largest tribe of Native Americans in Rhode Island.) In 1663, King Charles II of England gave Roger Williams a second charter for his colony that gave it a new name—the Colony of Rhode Island and Providence Plantations. No one is really sure where the name Rhode Island came from, although it might have been named after the Isle of Rhodes in the Aegean Sea.

Unlike the Massachusetts Bay Colony, in which everyone had to follow the rules of the Puritan church, in Providence settlers could worship in the church of their choice. Rhode Island was the last of the original thirteen colonies to formally approve the U.S. Constitution. Because so much of the state is coastline, it's called the Ocean State.

Coffee Milkshakes

In Rhode Island, you will see containers of coffee milk alongside containers of chocolate and white milk. Coffee-flavored syrup is used to flavor milk, milkshakes, and ice cream.

Time
10 minutes

Tools
ice cream scoop

blender

Makes
4 servings

Ingredients

1 cup brewed or instant coffee, cooled

1 cup 2% milk

1 tablespoon light vanilla syrup

3 scoops coffee ice cream

4 ice cubes

Steps

1. Put the coffee, milk, vanilla syrup, and ice cream in the blender. Mix well.

2. Add the ice cubes. Blend until the mixture is smooth.

3. Pour into 4 tall glasses.

Rhode Island Foods

Commercial fishing is very important in Rhode Island. Fishermen haul in tuna, striped bass, flounder, clams, and scallops. One tuna caught off the coast of Rhode Island can weigh close to 1,000 pounds. Poultry, eggs, and milk are important farm products.

Fabulous Food Festival
International Quahog Festival
North Kingstown
(October)

FUN FOOD FACTS

- Pilgrim women were the first to make a Rhode Island dish called johnnycakes, which are fried cornmeal cakes, something like pancakes. They were originally called "journey cakes" because they were small and easily portable.

- Rhode Islanders are masters of the clambake, which they learned from the Native Americans. The first step is to dig a hole in the sand or soil and line it with smooth rocks. Next, the rocks are heated up by building a fire on top of them and letting the fire burn for about an hour. Once the fire has burned out, a layer of seaweed is spread over the hot rocks and the clams are added and covered with more seaweed. The clams are steamed and ready to eat in about one hour. Other foods that are usually steamed along with the clams are lobster, baked potatoes, and corn on the cob.

- Quahogs are the largest size of hard-shelled clams you can buy, and they are very popular in Rhode Island.

- Rhode Island's state bird is a chicken called the Rhode Island Red. The breed, developed in Little Compton, became popular among poultry farmers because it lays lots of eggs and its meat is delicious. The Rhode Island Red even has its own monument, near Adamsville.

 VERMONT
The Green Mountain State

Capital: Montpelier

Other Major Cities: Burlington, Rutland

State Animal: Morgan Horse

State Bird: Hermit Thrush

State Insect: Honeybee

State Tree: Sugar Maple

State Flower: Red Clover

RED CLOVER

BURLINGTON

MONTPELIER

RUTLAND

HERMIT THRUSH

The word *Vermont* comes from two French words: *vert* meaning green, and *mont*, meaning mountain. The Green Mountains are a mountain chain that runs up the middle of the state. In addition to the mountains, the state has plenty of woodlands, and in autumn the trees put on a colorful foliage show.

The Lake Champlain region was originally settled by both the French and English. After the French and Indian War in 1763, the English took control of the Vermont territory. During English rule, Vermont was claimed by both the New York and the New Hampshire colonies. Shortly after the Revolutionary War started, Vermont became an independent republic, setting up its own government with its own constitution and adopting the name Vermont. Vermont even banned slavery in 1777. Vermont was admitted to the Union in 1791 as the fourteenth state.

Vermont Foods

Many of the trees in Vermont are sugar maples, from the sap of which maple syrup is made. Vermont produces the most maple syrup of any state in the country. Farms cover more than one-fifth of Vermont, and they mainly produce milk and many different apple varieties. Vermont is also known for its cheddar cheese.

Banana Berry Pancakes with Real Maple Syrup

Time
35 minutes

Tools
large bowl

wooden spoon

blender

rubber spatula

nonstick frying pan
or
griddle

tablespoon

spatula

Makes
16 to 18 3-inch
pancakes

Vermont farmers boil sap collected from sugar maple trees in buildings called sugarhouses until the sap is the consistency and sweetness of syrup. About 40 quarts of sap are needed to make 1 quart of maple syrup.

Ingredients

2 cups all-purpose flour

1 tablespoon baking powder

½ teaspoon ground nutmeg

½ teaspoon cinnamon

½ teaspoon salt

¼ cup sugar

2 small ripe bananas

1¼ cups milk

2 large eggs

1 teaspoon vanilla extract

⅓ cup canola oil

1 cup fresh strawberries, washed and sliced (or frozen sliced strawberries, thawed and drained)

vegetable oil cooking spray

Vermont maple syrup

Steps

1. In the large bowl, combine the flour, baking powder, nutmeg, cinnamon, salt, and sugar. Stir with the wooden spoon until the ingredients are well mixed.

2. Break the bananas into small pieces and put them in the blender. Blend at high speed until smooth.

3. Add the milk, eggs, and vanilla to the bananas. Blend again on high speed until smooth.

4. Pour the banana mixture into the bowl with the flour. Stir gently until just moistened.

5. Stir in the oil.

6. Fold in the strawberry slices with the rubber spatula.

7. Spray the nonstick griddle or frying pan with vegetable spray. Preheat on medium-high heat for 2 minutes or until hot.

8. Place 1 heaping tablespoon of pancake batter onto the griddle for each pancake.

9. Cook each pancake for about 2 minutes or until the surface is bubbly.

10. Using the spatula, flip each pancake and cook for 1½ minutes on the other side, or until it is lightly browned. Repeat with the rest of the batter. Serve hot with Vermont maple syrup.

FUN FOOD FACTS

- Montpelier biscuits, a type of cracker also known as "common crackers," were given that name because locals believed they had to be made with spring water from around Montpelier. The biscuits are creamy white and very crispy.

- The largest cheese manufacturer in Vermont is called the Cabot Creamery, located in Cabot, Vermont. This creamery is run by a cooperative of 500 milk producers. In 1930, the cooperative was producing too much milk, so they started making a variety of cheeses, including cheddar and Monterey Jack, as well as butter, cottage cheese, and spreads.

- Ben & Jerry's ice cream was first made in a small ice cream store in Burlington. Now it is made in a factory in Waterbury, and you can go there and take a tour.

Fabulous Food Festival

Vermont Maple Festival
St. Albans
(April)

PART 2

THE MIDDLE ATLANTIC

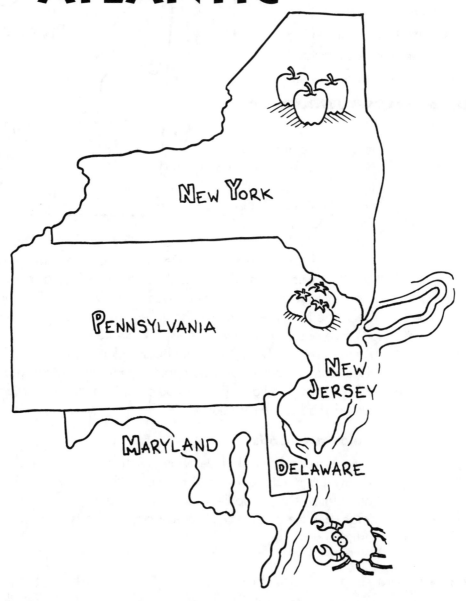

CHAPTER 7

DELAWARE
The First State

Capital: Dover

Other Major Cities: Newark, Wilmington

State Bird: Blue Hen Chicken

State Insect: Ladybug

State Tree: American Holly

State Flower: Peach Blossom

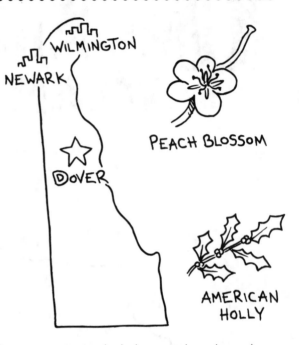

Delaware, the second smallest state, was the first state to approve the U.S. Constitution. That's why its nickname is the First State. In 1610 a British sea captain took shelter in a bay there during a storm. He named the bay De La Warr after the first colonial governor of Virginia, Thomas West, Lord De La Warr. The name came to be spelled Delaware and was also given to the Delaware River, to the Delaware Native Americans (also called the Lenape), and eventually to the state of Delaware. What is now Delaware was originally part of Pennsylvania. In 1776, when the British colonies joined to fight the Revolution, Delaware separated from Pennsylvania. Many years before 1776, Delaware had wanted to be an independent colony and in fact already had its own legislature.

Delaware Foods

Farms cover about half of Delaware. Many farms raise chickens, Delaware's most valuable farm product. Others grow fruits, vegetables, and grains, such as apples, corn, and wheat. The fishing industry is large, and the catch includes crabs, clams, oysters, sea bass, and weakfish, the state fish.

Classic Gingerbread Squares

Gingerbread is a dessert that Germans brought with them to Delaware.

Ingredients

vegetable oil cooking spray

¾ cup all-purpose flour

¾ cup whole wheat flour

½ cup light brown sugar

1 teaspoon cinnamon

1 teaspoon ground ginger

¼ teaspoon allspice

⅛ teaspoon ground cloves

½ teaspoon baking powder

½ teaspoon baking soda

½ cup shortening

½ cup dark molasses

½ cup water

1 large egg

⅓ cup coarsely chopped crystallized ginger

confectioner's sugar for dusting

Time
20 minutes to prepare
plus
35 to 40 minutes to bake

Tools
2-quart baking dish

large bowl

wooden spoon

medium bowl

electric mixer

oven mitts

kitchen scissors

Makes
12 servings

Steps

1. Preheat the oven to 350°F. Spray the baking dish with vegetable oil cooking spray.

2. In the large bowl, mix together with the wooden spoon the all-purpose flour, whole wheat flour, brown sugar, cinnamon, ginger, allspice, cloves, baking powder, and baking soda until well blended.

3. In the medium bowl, combine the shortening, molasses, water, and egg. Mix well.

4. Add the shortening mixture to the dry ingredients. With the electric mixer, beat for 2 to 3 minutes on low speed.

5. When well combined, beat the mixture on high speed for 3 minutes or until smooth.

6. Fold in the ginger. Pour the batter into the prepared baking dish.

7. Bake for 35 to 40 minutes or until the center springs back when touched lightly.

8. Cool completely. Cut the gingerbread into squares. Sprinkle with confectioner's sugar.

FUN FOOD FACTS

- A woman named Cecil Steel, of Ocean View, accidentally started the state's huge chicken industry in 1923. Instead of receiving the 50 chicks she had ordered to provide eggs and meat for her family, she received 500 chicks. She kept them, and decided to butcher and market these chickens when they were sixteen weeks old, which was considered early at that time. She called her chickens "broilers" because they could be cooked quickly. Within ten years, the broiler industry (broilers are now defined as chickens between nine and twelve weeks of age) was firmly established in Delaware.

- More bananas enter our country through the port in Wilmington than through any other port in the United States.

Fabulous Food Festival
Rockwood's Victorian Ice Cream Festival
Wilmington (July)

CHAPTER 8

MARYLAND
The Old Line State

Capital: Annapolis

Other Major Cities: Baltimore, Silver Spring

State Animal: Chesapeake Bay Retriever

State Bird: Baltimore Oriole

State Insect: Baltimore Checkerspot Butterfly

State Tree: White Oak

State Flower: Black-eyed Susan

BALTIMORE

SILVER SPRING

ANNAPOLIS

BALTIMORE ORIOLE

CHESAPEAKE BAY RETRIEVER

In 1632, King Charles I granted a charter to the second Lord Baltimore, Cecil Calvert, for the land along the Chesapeake Bay and north of the Potomac River. The king asked that the colony be named after his wife, Henrietta Maria, so it became Maryland. Maryland was one of the original thirteen colonies.

Because of the stubborn courage of Maryland soldiers in the Continental Line, the line of soldiers who fought during the Revolutionary War, Maryland earned its nickname, the Old Line State. Three years after ratifying the U.S. Constitution, Maryland donated land on the Potomac River to become the nation's capital, Washington, D.C.

Maryland Foods

Most of Maryland's food products come from the Chesapeake Bay, including crabs, clams, and oysters. As in Delaware, poultry is Maryland's primary agricultural product. Maryland also produces milk, apples, and tomatoes.

Maryland Baked Crab Cakes

Time
20 minutes to prepare
plus
12 to 15 minutes to bake

Tools
9-inch square baking pan

cutting board

sharp knife

nonstick skillet

small bowl

large bowl

shallow baking dish

oven mitts

Makes
4 large or 6 medium
crab cakes

Crabs are used in many dishes such as crab soups, crab salads, and the famous crab cakes.

Ingredients

vegetable oil cooking spray

4 scallions

½ green pepper

2 teaspoons olive oil

2 tablespoons sliced pimientos, drained

⅔ cup seasoned bread crumbs

¼ teaspoon paprika

1 teaspoon dried parsley

1 pound lump crab meat, shell pieces and cartilage removed

1 teaspoon soy sauce

3 to 4 tablespoons mayonnaise

Steps

1. Preheat the oven to 450°F. Spray the baking pan with vegetable oil cooking spray. Set aside.

2. Wash and dry the scallions. On the cutting board with the sharp knife, slice the white part of the scallion into ¼-inch pieces. Discard the root end.

3. Wash the pepper and pat dry. Using the knife, trim the white ribs out of the inside of the pepper. On the cutting board, cut the pepper into ¼-inch-wide strips. Cut each strip into small pieces.

4. Put the olive oil in the nonstick skillet and heat on medium heat for two minutes. Sauté the scallions, peppers, and pimientos until soft and translucent.

5. In the small bowl, mix together the bread crumbs, paprika, and parsley until well blended.

6. In the large bowl, mix together the crab meat, sautéed scallions, peppers, pimientos, and 1 tablespoon of the bread crumb mixture. Add the soy sauce and mayonnaise and mix well.

7. Form the mixture into 4 to 6 flat crab cakes.

8. Pour the remaining bread crumb mixture into the shallow baking dish.

9. Coat the crab cakes on all sides with the bread crumb mixture.

10. Place the crab cakes in the prepared 9-inch baking pan. Bake for 12 to 15 minutes or until the cakes are golden brown.

FUN FOOD FACTS

- The Chesapeake Bay's blue crabs are excellent crabs for cooking. They are called blue crabs because the underside of the crab's large claws is blue. The blue crab sheds its shell over twenty times during its lifetime of about three years.

- More than 200 years ago, Maryland cooks invented beaten biscuits. Once the biscuit dough was made, it was beaten with a hammer or ax for 30 minutes. This made the biscuits light and airy.

Fabulous Food Festival
National Hard Crab Derby and Fair
Chrisfield
(September)

YE OLDE BEATEN BISCUIT MIX

CHAPTER 9

NEW JERSEY
The Garden State

Capital: Trenton

Other Major Cities: Atlantic City, Newark

State Animal: Horse

State Bird: Eastern Goldfinch

State Insect: Honeybee

State Tree: Red Oak

State Flower: Purple Violet

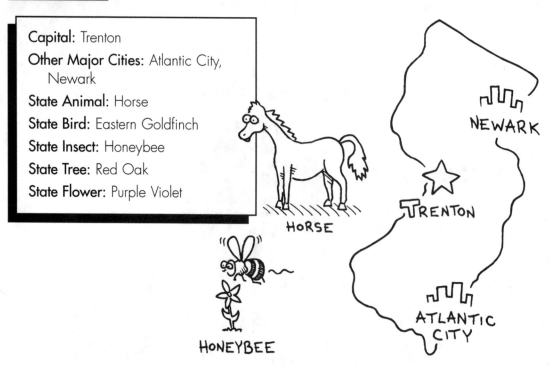

HORSE

HONEYBEE

NEWARK

TRENTON

ATLANTIC CITY

The Dutch and Swedes were the first white settlers in what is now northern New Jersey. The English won control of these lands in 1664, and shortly after, King Charles II of England gave the land, along with the rest of what is now New Jersey, to his brother James. James named the area New Jersey in honor of Sir George Carteret, who had served as the Governor of Jersey, an island in the English Channel, and later gave Carteret and another lord the land. New Jersey was one of the original thirteen colonies, and was known as the "Crossroads of the Revolution" because it was the scene of so many battles. Its nickname, the Garden State, comes from its large number of vegetable farms and fruit orchards.

Italian Submarine Sandwiches

Italian subs include tasty Italian meats, such as prosciutto (a spicy ham) and salami, and Italian cheeses, such as provolone and mozzarella. Submarine sandwiches (sandwiches served on long Italian rolls) go by different names, depending on which part of the country you are in. For example, in Pennsylvania they are called hoagies, in New York they are called heroes, and in Massachusetts they are called grinders. No matter what you call them, they make a great lunch!

Time
15 minutes

Tools
cutting board

knife

spoon

Makes
4 sandwiches

Ingredients

¼ head iceberg lettuce

1 large tomato

1 small onion

4 individual submarine (long) rolls

4 tablespoons oil

4 tablespoons vinegar

6 ounces sliced prosciutto or ham

6 ounces sliced salami

6 ounces sliced provolone or mozzarella

Steps

1. Wash the lettuce and tomato and pat dry.

2. On the cutting board, slice the lettuce and tomato.

3. Remove the papery skin from the onion. Cut the onion in half. Lay each half flat on the cutting board and cut into ¼-inch slices.

4. Split the rolls in half horizontally.

5. With the spoon, drizzle 1 tablespoon of oil and 1 tablespoon of vinegar inside each roll.

6. Keeping each roll open, place a few slices of prosciutto, salami, and cheese on both sides.

7. Layer lettuce, tomatoes, and onions on top of the meat and cheese.

8. Using the knife to push the vegetables into the sandwich, close the rolls. Cut each roll in half and serve.

New Jersey Foods

With such rich soil in central and southern New Jersey, these parts of the state are known for growing quality vegetables and fruits, such as blueberries, peaches, apples, spinach, asparagus, and squash. New Jersey is a top state for producing tomatoes, which are essential summer fare in New Jersey, New York, and other states as well. With its busy Atlantic coastline, New Jersey is also known for its fruits of the sea—clams, crabs, oysters, and fluke, to name a few.

FUN FOOD FACTS

- In 1897, John Dorrance did a food experiment that resulted in the technology used to condense soups for canning. He founded the Campbell Soup Company, which is still based in Camden and includes a Soup Tureen Museum.

- In 1904, near Princeton, the first quart of pasteurized milk was produced. The process of pasteurization, invented by the Frenchman Louis Pasteur, removes harmful bacteria.

- Asparagus has been grown in southern New Jersey since colonial times.

Fabulous Food Festival
New Jersey Seafood Festival
Belmar
(June)

NEW YORK
The Empire State

Capital: Albany

Other Major Cities:
Buffalo, New York City

State Animal: Beaver

State Bird: Red-breasted Bluebird

State Tree: Sugar Maple

State Flower: Rose

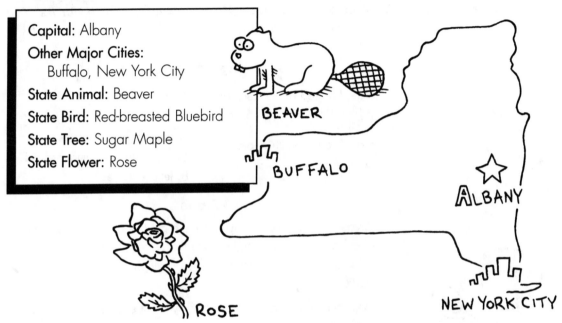

Originally called New Netherlands by the Dutch, the colony was renamed New York by the British in honor of James, the Duke of York, when they captured it in 1664. New York was one of the original thirteen colonies and the site of many Revolutionary War battles. When the federal Constitution was adopted, New York City was chosen to be the nation's capital. George Washington, the first president, was inaugurated in New York City in 1789. Earlier, in 1784, during a tour of New York, George Washington referred to the state as the "Seat of Empire," so its nickname became the Empire State.

New York Foods

Dairy products, including milk and cheese, bring the most money for farmers. Other farm products include cattle and crops such as vegetables, grapes, and apples, the state fruit. European settlers introduced apples in the 1600s.

Time
25 minutes

Tools
knife

cutting board

large bowl

wooden spoon

Makes
4 servings

Waldorf Salad was created by the maitre d'hotel of the famous Waldorf Astoria Hotel in New York City for its grand opening in 1893.

Ingredients

1 large, firm red apple, such as Cortland, Empire, or Red Delicious

1 large Granny Smith apple

1 tablespoon lemon juice

4 stalks celery

½ cup raisins

¼ cup chopped walnuts

¼ cup reduced-fat mayonnaise

8 lettuce leaves

Steps

1. Wash the apples. Using the knife on the cutting board, cut the apples in half and remove the seeds. Cut the apples into ½-inch cubes and place in the bowl. Sprinkle with lemon juice.

2. Remove any celery leaves and wash the celery. Slice the celery into ¼-inch slices.

3. Combine the apples, celery, raisins, walnuts, and mayonnaise. Mix well with the wooden spoon.

4. Wash and pat dry the lettuce leaves. Place 2 lettuce leaves on each serving plate. Divide the salad into 4 equal servings, placing each serving on the lettuce leaves. Serve immediately.

FUN FOOD FACTS

- Shredded wheat cereal was first made in 1892 by Henry Perky in Watertown. He built a machine that could press wheat into shredded strips. When baked, the strips became quite tasty. He eventually moved his business, the Shredded Wheat Company, to Niagara Falls and in 1918 it was acquired by Nabisco.

- The Big Apple was first used as a nickname for New York City by touring jazz musicians of the 1930s, who used the word *apple* to mean any town or city. Playing in New York City was playing the big apple!

- The New York cheesecake, which is distinguished by a smooth cream-cheese filling baked in a graham cracker crust, was popularized in the 1940s by Lindy's restaurant. Today, it can be found on restaurant menus throughout the country.

Fabulous Food Festival

Oyster Festival
Oyster Bay
(October)

CHAPTER 11

PENNSYLVANIA
The Keystone State

Capital: Harrisburg
Other Major Cities:
Philadelphia, Pittsburgh
State Animal:
White-tailed Deer
State Bird: Ruffed Grouse
State Tree: Hemlock
State Flower:
Mountain Laurel

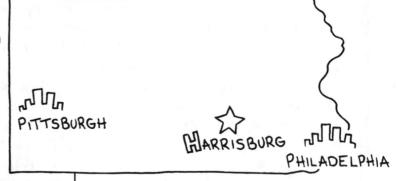

MOUNTAIN LAUREL

RUFFED GROUSE

The fifth largest state, Pennsylvania, which means "Penn's Woods," was given by Charles II of England to William Penn as payment of a debt owed to Penn's father, Admiral William Penn. William Penn was a Quaker, a member of the Religious Society of Friends. Pennsylvania, one of the original thirteen colonies, played a major role in the development of our country. It was in Philadelphia that the First Continental Congress met and the Declaration of Independence was signed in 1776. Philadelphia was the capital of the United States from 1790 to 1800. Pennsylvania is known as the Keystone State because it formed the center, or keystone, of the arch formed by the original thirteen colonies.

Pennsylvania Foods

Pennsylvania is the nation's leading producer of mushrooms. Dairy products and cattle are also important farm products, along with buckwheat, corn, vegetables, grapes, and orchard fruits such as apples.

•••• Philadelphia Soft Pretzels ••••

During the 1700s and early 1800s, many German immigrants, especially farmers, settled in Pennsylvania. They became known as the Pennsylvania "Deutsch" (which means "German"), but eventually "Deutsch" was mispronounced so often that it became "Dutch." The Pennsylvania Dutch contributed a wide variety of distinctive foods, such as sauerkraut, rye bread, apple butter, and pretzels. On the streets of Philadelphia, you can buy big, warm, soft pretzels that make a great snack. Philadelphians eat their soft pretzels with mustard.

Time
30 minutes to prepare
plus
45 minutes rising time
plus
12 to 15 minutes
to bake

Tools
large bowl

wooden spoon

pastry board

pastry brush

medium bowl

kitchen towel

cookie sheets

oven mitts

Makes
24 pretzels

Ingredients

2 packages active dry yeast

1½ cups warm water

2 tablespoons sugar

1 teaspoon salt

2 cups whole wheat flour

1¾ cups all-purpose flour

1 teaspoon olive oil

1 large egg, beaten

sesame seeds

Steps

1. Preheat the oven to 425°F.

2. Stir the yeast and warm water together in the bowl with the wooden spoon. Make sure the water is not too hot!

3. Add the sugar and salt and mix well.

4. Add the flours to the bowl in small amounts and stir well after each addition. Mix with the wooden spoon, stirring constantly until the mixture forms into a dough.

5. Turn the dough out onto a lightly floured pastry board or very clean countertop and knead the dough for 5 minutes. To knead, press the dough out with your hands, then fold it in half. Give the dough a quarter turn after each fold and start again.

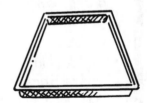

6. Using the pastry brush, brush the medium bowl with olive oil. Place the dough into the bowl and cover with the kitchen towel. Place in a draft-free spot, such as your oven or microwave (don't turn it on!) and allow the dough to rise for 45 minutes.

7. Cut off pieces of dough and roll into ropes about 12 inches long. Shape each rope into the traditional pretzel shape and place on ungreased cookie sheets. Leave about 2 inches of space around each pretzel.

8. Brush each pretzel with egg and then sprinkle with sesame seeds.

9. Bake for 12 to 15 minutes or until golden in color.

FUN FOOD FACTS

- In 1900, Milton Hershey sold his caramel factory in Lancaster, Pennsylvania, and returned to his birthplace, Derry Church, to start a chocolate factory. In 1903 he set up what would become the world's largest chocolate manufacturing plant. Today, Hershey's plant is surrounded by the town that bears its name, as well as a popular theme park.

- A popular Pennsylvania Dutch food is shoofly pie. Shoofly pie is made by turning a crumb-cake mixture sweetened with molasses into a pie shell and baking it. It got its name because supposedly you had to shoo the flies away while it was cooling.

- Philadelphia is not only the birthplace of our country, but it is also the birthplace of the ice cream soda. It was invented in Philadelphia in 1874 when Robert M. Green ran out of sweet cream for a drink that also used syrup and carbonated water. He substituted ice cream for the sweet cream, and the first ice cream sodas were a big hit!

Fabulous Food Festival
Bean Soup Festival
McClure
(September)

PART 3

THE SOUTH

CHAPTER 12

ALABAMA
The Heart of Dixie

Capital: Montgomery

Other Major Cities: Birmingham, Mobile

State Bird: Yellow-shafted Flicker

State Insect: Monarch Butterfly

State Tree: Southern Pine

State Flower: Camellia

BIRMINGHAM

MONTGOMERY

MOBILE

YELLOW-SHAFTED FLICKER

CAMELLIA

Alabama got its name from the Alibamu Indians. The French were the first to establish a permanent settlement in Alabama in 1702. The United States took control of the area in 1813, and in 1819, Alabama became the twenty-second state in the union. Alabama is nicknamed the Heart of Dixie because it is in the center of the South, which is sometimes called Dixieland or Dixie. Alabama is also nicknamed the Cotton State because cotton was at one time its biggest crop. It is still a leading cotton producer.

Alabama Foods

Much livestock is raised in Alabama, including beef cattle, chickens, and hogs. Farmers grow wheat, oats, sweet potatoes, peanuts, and pecans. Bees are raised for their honey and wax. Commercial fishing boats in the Gulf of Mexico bring in red snapper, flounder, shrimp, and crabs.

···· Sweet Potato Biscuits ····

Sweet potatoes are grown in Alabama and appear on many menus. The sweet potato has had other names in the past, including Indian potato, long potato, and tuckahoe. Native Americans used sweet potatoes and they taught settlers how to grow and use the vegetable.

Ingredients

vegetable oil cooking spray

1¾ cups all-purpose flour

4 teaspoons baking powder

1¼ teaspoons salt

½ teaspoon cinnamon

½ teaspoon ground nutmeg

¼ teaspoon ground cloves

¼ cup chopped pecans

2 cups canned sweet potatoes or yams

½ cup sugar

¼ cup light brown sugar

1 teaspoon vanilla extract

½ cup margarine

butter

honey

Time
15 minutes to prepare
plus
12 to 14 minutes to bake

Tools
cookie sheet

large bowl

small bowl

fork

medium bowl

pastry blender

wooden spoon

cutting board

rolling pin

3-inch biscuit cutter

spatula

oven mitts

Makes
16 biscuits

Steps

1. Preheat the oven to 350°F. Spray the cookie sheet with vegetable oil cooking spray.

2. In the large bowl, mix together the flour, baking powder, salt, cinnamon, nutmeg, cloves, and pecans. In the small bowl, mash the sweet potatoes with a fork.

3. Combine the sweet potatoes, sugar, brown sugar, and vanilla in the medium bowl. Set aside.

4. Cut the margarine into small pieces and blend into the flour mixture with the pastry blender, using a back-and-forth motion until the mixture resembles small peas.

5. Add the sweet potato mixture to the flour mixture and stir thoroughly with the wooden spoon.

6. Turn the dough out onto a lightly floured cutting board and knead for about 5 minutes until well blended.

7. Roll the dough to ½-inch thickness. Cut the dough with a 3-inch biscuit cutter and place biscuits 2 inches apart on the cookie sheet.

8. Bake for 12 to 14 minutes or until golden brown.

9. Remove the cookie sheet from the oven. Let it cool for 2 minutes, then remove the biscuits with the spatula. Serve with butter and honey.

FUN FOOD FACTS

- Fried pies are a specialty of Alabama. Fried pies are made by filling pie dough, often with peaches or peach butter, then folding the dough into a half-moon shape, and frying it in fat.

- George Washington Carver (1864–1943) was an African American agricultural scientist who did much research on peanuts at Tuskegee Institute (now Tuskegee University) in Alabama. He found over 300 uses for peanuts, including using peanuts to make a milk substitute and soap.

Fabulous Food
Festival
National Shrimp Festival
Gulf Shores
(October)

CHAPTER 13

ARKANSAS
The Land of Opportunity

Capital: Little Rock

Other Major Cities: Fayetteville, Fort Smith

State Bird: Mockingbird

State Tree: Pine

State Flower: Apple Blossom

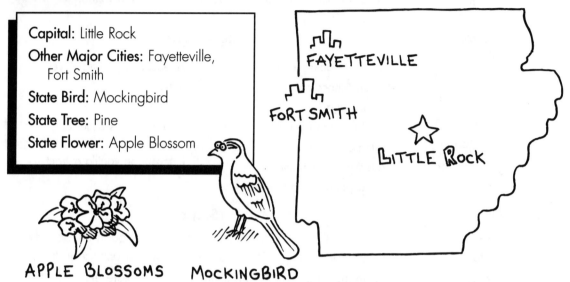

FAYETTEVILLE

FORT SMITH

☆ LITTLE ROCK

APPLE BLOSSOMS   MOCKINGBIRD

The name Arkansas comes from the name French explorers gave to a tribe of Native Americans they encountered. In 1682, the French explorer La Salle claimed the Mississippi Valley (including what is now Arkansas) for France and named it Louisiana after the king of France, Louis XIV. In 1686, Henri de Tonti, The "Father of Arkansas," established the first European settlement with only six residents. Few settlers came there over the next hundred years. There were only 386 whites living in Arkansas in 1799. In 1803, France sold the land called Louisiana to the United States. By 1819, many settlers from crowded Eastern states had moved to Arkansas, and Arkansas became a territory. In 1836, with about 60,000 residents, Arkansas became the twenty-fifth state. In order to attract even more people, Arkansas called itself the Land of Opportunity.

Arkansas Foods

Arkansas leads the country in producing chickens and growing rice. Farmers also plant wheat, grapes, snap beans, tomatoes, and pecans. Many also raise beef cattle, dairy cattle, and turkeys.

Chocolate Rice Pudding

Here's a tasty way to cook some Arkansas rice.

Time
20 minutes

Tools
medium saucepan

small saucepan

medium bowl

wooden spoon

double boiler

egg separator

cup

small bowl

wire whip

fork

Makes
6 servings

Ingredients

½ cup uncooked rice

2 cups chocolate milk

¾ cup sugar

1 tablespoon flour

¼ teaspoon salt

¼ teaspoon cinnamon

¼ teaspoon ground nutmeg

⅛ teaspoon ground cloves

water

3 large eggs

2 tablespoons butter or margarine

1 teaspoon vanilla extract

Steps

1. Using the medium saucepan, prepare enough uncooked rice to make 1 cup of cooked rice, following package instructions.

2. In the small saucepan, simmer the chocolate milk until it begins to steam, about 3 minutes.

3. In the medium bowl, mix together the sugar, flour, salt, cinnamon, nutmeg, and cloves with a wooden spoon. Pour in the milk and stir until well blended.

4. Put 2 inches of water in the bottom of the double boiler. Put the chocolate milk mixture in the top of the double boiler and cook on medium-high heat until it begins to boil. Allow the mixture to boil for 2 minutes. Turn the heat to low.

5. Cover the mixture and cook for about 5 to 7 minutes on low heat, stirring occasionally.

6. Separate the egg yolks from the egg whites in the cup. Freeze the egg whites for another recipe.

7. Place 4 to 5 tablespoons of the hot milk mixture in the small bowl. Allow it to cool slightly for about 2 minutes. Vigorously whisk the egg yolks into it.

8. Whisk the egg mixture into the chocolate milk mixture in the double boiler. Cook on low heat for about 5 minutes, covered, stirring occasionally.

9. Remove the double boiler from the heat. Stir the rice with a fork and add it to the mixture in the double boiler. Blend in the butter and vanilla. Cover again and set pudding aside to cool slightly, about 10 minutes. Serve warm, or refrigerate and serve cold.

FUN FOOD FACTS

- The world's biggest watermelons come from Hope. Farmers have grown watermelons as big as 260 pounds. In Hope, you will also find watermelon-eating and seed-spitting contests. The seed-spitting record is 30 feet.
- The pink tomato grown in southern Arkansas is both the state fruit and the state vegetable. The tomato is really a fruit, but most people think of it as a vegetable.

Fabulous Food Festival
Hope Watermelon Festival
Hope (August)

CHAPTER 14

FLORIDA
The Sunshine State

Capital: Tallahassee

Other Major Cities:
Jacksonville, Miami

State Animals: Manatee, Porpoise

State Bird: Mockingbird

State Tree: Sabal Palm

State Flower: Orange Blossom

State Drink: Orange Juice

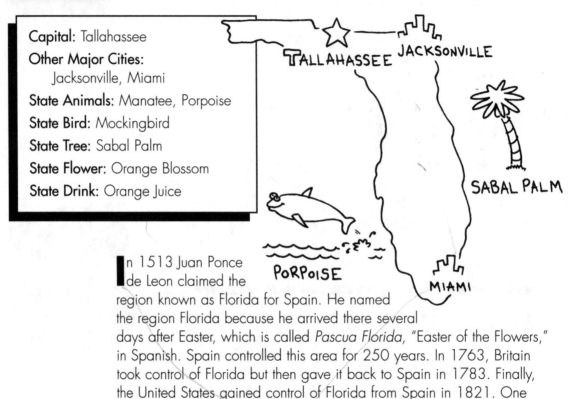

In 1513 Juan Ponce de Leon claimed the region known as Florida for Spain. He named the region Florida because he arrived there several days after Easter, which is called *Pascua Florida*, "Easter of the Flowers," in Spanish. Spain controlled this area for 250 years. In 1763, Britain took control of Florida but then gave it back to Spain in 1783. Finally, the United States gained control of Florida from Spain in 1821. One year later Florida became a territory, and in 1845, it became the twenty-seventh state. Florida's nickname, the Sunshine State, expresses well the climate in this state—generally warm and sunny year-round.

Florida Foods

Florida is this country's number one producer of citrus fruits, such as oranges, grapefruits, lemons, and limes. Because the state has warm weather and plentiful rain, Florida farmers can grow many fruits and vegetables. A few also raise beef and dairy cattle. Commercial fishing boats bring in lots of seafood, especially shrimp and lobster.

Sugar cane was brought to Florida by the Spanish conquistadors in the sixteenth century. Here they established plantations to grow the valuable crop.

California grows most of the lemons in the United States, but Florida grows the most limes. The Key lime is a unique type of lime that grows only on the Florida Keys, a string of tiny islands off the southern tip of the state. The Key lime is yellow on the outside and green on the inside. Key limes are now grown in small gardens because a hurricane destroyed all of the major lime groves. Key lime seeds are believed to have been brought here by Columbus.

Time
15 minutes to prepare
plus
15 minutes to bake

Tools
egg separator

2 medium bowls

wire whip

electric mixer

sandwich spreader

Makes
1 9-inch pie

Ingredients

4 large eggs

1 14-ounce can sweetened condensed milk

½ cup bottled Key lime juice

1 9-inch prepared graham cracker pie shell

1 cup heavy cream for whipping

Steps

1. Preheat the oven to 350°F.

2. Use the egg separator to separate the egg yolks from the egg whites. Put the yolks in a medium bowl. Freeze the egg whites for another recipe.

3. Whisk the egg yolks for 3 minutes.

4. Add the condensed milk and lime juice and continue to whisk.

5. Pour the mixture into the prepared shell. Bake for 15 minutes or until the center of the pie is set. Cool completely.

6. Make the whipped cream by beating the cream in the other bowl with an electric mixer on high speed. This takes about 2 to 3 minutes. Do not overbeat. Spread a thin layer on top of the pie with the sandwich spreader.

7. Serve immediately or refrigerate.

FUN FOOD FACTS

- Orange trees were introduced to the St. Augustine area over 500 years ago by the Spanish. Lemons and grapefruits came much later.

- Unusual food products from Florida include alligator meat and frogs' legs. Both have a mild flavor. Alligator can be made into anything from alligator sausages to sweet-and-sour alligator.

- In a Florida restaurant, you may find a salad called "palm hearts." Palm hearts are taken from Florida's state tree, the sabal palm. They are considered a tropical delicacy, and are quite expensive.

Fabulous Food Festival
Florida Citrus Festival
Winter Haven
(February)

SWEET & SOUR ALLIGATOR

CHAPTER 15

GEORGIA
The Peach State

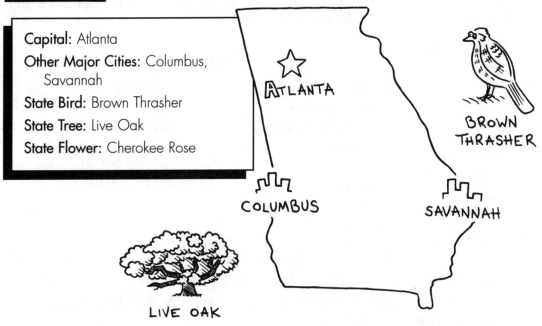

Capital: Atlanta

Other Major Cities: Columbus, Savannah

State Bird: Brown Thrasher

State Tree: Live Oak

State Flower: Cherokee Rose

ATLANTA

COLUMBUS

SAVANNAH

BROWN THRASHER

LIVE OAK

The Georgia colony was settled in 1733 by the English general James Edward Oglethorpe and a ragtag group of families that he had rescued from debtor's prison in England. King George II, who thought the colony would act as a buffer between South Carolina and the Spanish colony of Florida, granted the charter for the colony (named after the king, of course) in 1732. The struggling colonists received help from the Yamacraw Indians, and soon more settlers arrived. In 1752 Georgia became one of the original thirteen colonies. The state's nickname, of course, comes from the fact that lots of peaches are grown there.

Georgia Foods

Georgia is especially well known for growing peanuts and peaches. Farmers also grow pecans, grapes, apples, cabbage, and corn. Georgia is a leading producer of chickens and eggs.

···· Peanutty Peanut Butter ···· and Banana Bread

Time
20 minutes to prepare plus
70 minutes to bake

Tools
9 x 5 x 3-inch loaf pan

2 medium bowls

wooden spoon

small bowl

fork

oven mitts

wire rack

Makes
1 loaf

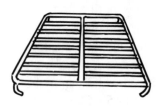

Georgia peanuts make this bread out of this world! Enjoy as a dessert or snack.

Ingredients

vegetable oil cooking spray

2 cups all-purpose flour

1 teaspoon baking soda

½ teaspoon salt

½ cup shortening

1 cup smooth peanut butter

⅔ cup light brown sugar

2 large eggs

2 ripe bananas

1 teaspoon lemon juice

½ cup crushed dry-roasted unsalted peanuts

1 teaspoon vanilla

Steps

1. Preheat the oven to 350°F. Spray the loaf pan with vegetable oil cooking spray. Set aside.

2. In a medium bowl, stir together the flour, baking soda, and salt.

3. In the other medium bowl, beat the shortening, peanut butter, and brown sugar together with the wooden spoon until the mixture is smooth and creamy, about 2 minutes.

4. Add the eggs to the peanut butter mixture and continue beating until well blended.

5. In the small bowl, mash the bananas with a fork until smooth. Mix in the lemon juice. Set aside.

6. Stir the flour mixture into the peanut butter mixture just until moistened. Add the bananas and vanilla. Fold in the peanuts.

7. Pour the batter into the loaf pan. Bake for 1 hour and 10 minutes or until the center springs back when lightly touched.

8. Cool for 20 minutes on the wire rack before removing from pan.

FUN FOOD FACTS

- The first Coca-Cola was sold in a drugstore in Atlanta in 1886. Like Pepsi-Cola, Coca-Cola was first sold as a remedy for headaches. Coca-Cola is still headquartered in Atlanta.

- Georgia grows more peanuts than any other state. That's why it is sometimes called the Goober State. Goober is an African word for peanut.

- Europeans did not bring peanuts to the United States. Peanuts, along with pecans and black walnuts, are native to our continent.

- The world's largest drive-in restaurant, the Varsity, is in Atlanta. It has been serving burgers since 1928.

Fabulous Food
Festival
**Vidalia Onion
Festival**
Vidalia
(May)

CHAPTER 16

KENTUCKY
The Bluegrass State

Capital: Frankfort
Other Major Cities: Lexington, Louisville
State Bird: Cardinal
State Tree: Kentucky Coffee
State Flower: Goldenrod

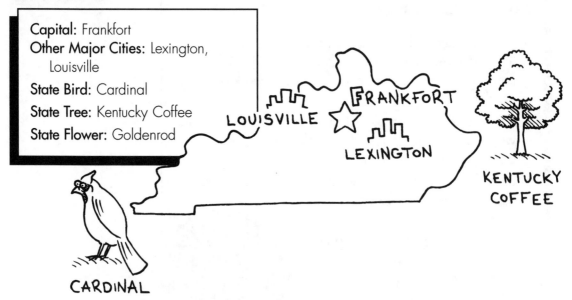

LOUISVILLE

FRANKFORT

LEXINGTON

KENTUCKY COFFEE

CARDINAL

Native Americans and early European settlers called this region Kentucky, which was spelled Kentucke until 1792. Although no one is really sure what the name means, it may come from an Iroquois word meaning "great meadows." Parts of Kentucky are covered with a type of dark, lush grass called bluegrass because in the spring it has bluish-purple buds that make entire fields look blue when they bloom.

The first European settlers were English. Many of the early pioneers traveling into Kentucky crossed the Appalachian Mountains at the eastern end of the state. Daniel Boone, Kentucky's most famous early pioneer, was hired to make a trail across these mountains. After the Revolutionary War, in 1783, Kentucky became a county of Virginia. However, in 1792, Kentucky decided to join the new Union on its own and was welcomed as the fifteenth state.

Kentucky Foods

Foods grown in Kentucky include corn, dairy products, and soybeans. Apples, peaches, and popcorn are also grown.

Burgoo, a stew made with chicken, beef, vegetables, and curry, is probably the most famous dish from Kentucky. The origin of the name is uncertain, but we do know that this dish dates back to frontier days, when it often was made with deer and squirrel meat.

Ingredients

3 cups water

1 cup chicken broth, homemade or canned

2 cups canned crushed tomatoes

¾ pound chicken tenders or strips

¾ pound stew beef, cubed

3 medium boiling potatoes

1 medium onion

1 cup frozen lima beans

1 cup frozen corn

1 10-ounce package frozen cut okra

1 cup frozen sliced carrots

2 teaspoons curry powder

1 teaspoon sugar

½ teaspoon pepper

Time
2 hours

Tools
4½-quart heavy, covered baking dish

cutting board

knife

slotted spoon

peeler

Makes
6 servings

Steps

1. Combine the water, chicken stock, and crushed tomatoes in the baking dish and bring to a boil. Reduce the heat and simmer for 15 minutes.

2. Meanwhile, cut the chicken tenders into 1-inch pieces.

3. Add the beef and chicken pieces to the pot and simmer, covered, for 1 hour. Remove the chicken with the slotted spoon. Set aside.

4. Peel the potatoes and cut them into cubes. Place them in the pot.

5. Remove the papery skin from the onion. On a cutting board with a sharp knife, cut the onion in half. Lay the onion halves cut-side down on the cutting board and chop.

6. Add the lima beans, corn, okra, carrots, curry powder, sugar, and pepper to the pot. Return the mixture to boiling, then reduce heat.

7. Simmer, covered, about 25 minutes, or until all vegetables are cooked through and tender. Put the chicken back in the pot. Cook an additional 5 minutes to warm up the chicken.

FUN FOOD FACTS

- In 1934, the first cheeseburger in the United States was served at Kaelin's Restaurant in Louisville, Kentucky.
- At the age of sixty-five, "Colonel" Harland Sanders set off on a trip around the country to sell restaurants the right to use his special preparation technique and secret seasoning mix to make what is now called KFC (Kentucky Fried Chicken). Restaurants paid him five cents for each order they served to customers. On a television cooking show with the first restaurant owner to make his product, Sanders decided to dress like an old-fashioned Kentucky colonel, with a pure white suit and a goatee, to attract sales.

Fabulous Food
Festival
**International
Bar-B-Q Festival**
Owensboro
(May)

CHAPTER 17

OUISIANA
The Pelican State

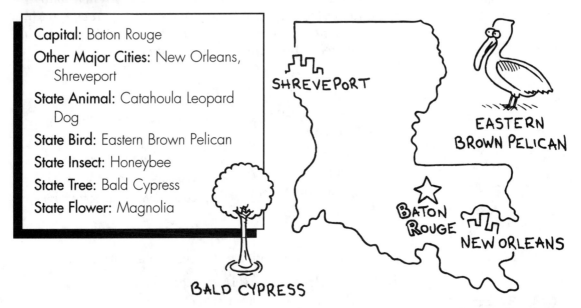

Capital: Baton Rouge

Other Major Cities: New Orleans, Shreveport

State Animal: Catahoula Leopard Dog

State Bird: Eastern Brown Pelican

State Insect: Honeybee

State Tree: Bald Cypress

State Flower: Magnolia

SHREVEPORT

EASTERN BROWN PELICAN

BATON ROUGE

NEW ORLEANS

BALD CYPRESS

In 1682, the French explorer La Salle claimed the Mississippi Valley for France and named it Louisiana in honor of King Louis XIV. At that time, the Louisiana Territory stretched from the Mississippi River to the Rocky Mountains and as far north as Canada. By 1762, France gave Louisiana to Spain because maintaining colonies was too costly. Louisiana prospered under Spanish rule, so much in fact that France persuaded Spain to return it to France in 1800. Only three years later, in 1803, the United States bought the Louisiana Territory from France for $15 million, and the area was split up into territories to make it easier to govern. Much of what is now Louisiana was named the Territory of Orleans. In 1812, the Territory of Orleans was renamed Louisiana and became the eighteenth state. The state is nicknamed the Pelican State after the eastern brown pelican.

Louisiana Foods

Local seafood, such as oysters, crawfish, and shrimp are abundant in Louisiana and influence all styles of cooking. Other important products include chicken, seasonal game, red peppers, and garlic.

Time
15 minutes

Tools
knife

cutting board

shallow bowl

wire whip

paring knife

nonstick skillet

spatula

Makes
4 servings

Pain perdu *is French for "lost bread." The French who came to Louisiana from Canada brought this recipe with them. It is similar to French toast. The original pain perdu was flavored with orange-flower water.*

Ingredients

1 12-inch-long loaf of day-old French bread

¾ cup milk

2 large eggs

1 tablespoon confectioner's sugar

3 tablespoons orange juice

1 teaspoon vanilla extract

1 cup fresh strawberries

vegetable oil cooking spray

confectioner's sugar for dusting

Steps

1. Cut the French bread into 8 slices on the cutting board.

2. In the shallow bowl, whisk together the milk, eggs, sugar, orange juice, and vanilla extract.

3. Wash the strawberries and pat dry. Use the paring knife to remove the green stems, then slice the berries.

4. Dip the slices of bread into the milk and egg mixture so that the bread soaks up some of the mixture.

5. Spray the skillet with vegetable oil cooking spray. Preheat on medium for 2 minutes.

6. Fry the soaked bread pieces until golden on one side; about 2 minutes. Turn the bread over and fry the second side for about 1 to 1½ minutes.

7. Serve sliced strawberries on top of the *pain perdu* and dust with confectioner's sugar.

FUN FOOD FACTS

- Southern Louisiana is home to descendants of the original French and Spanish settlers, called Creoles, as well as descendants of French settlers from the Acadia region of eastern Canada, called Cajuns. Both the Creoles and Cajuns have their own styles of cooking. Typical Creole dishes include spicy stews served with rice, such as gumbo and jambalaya. Typical Cajun dishes include red beans and rice, and boudin, which is a spicy sausage.

- On Avery Island, the McIlhenny family developed Tabasco sauce, a sauce made with hot peppers. The sauce is named after the river and town in southern Mexico from which the peppers originally came.

- Every other year, the town of Breaux Bridge has a crawfish festival, which includes a crawfish-eating contest and a crawfish race! The design of the crawfish racetrack takes into account that crawfish don't crawl in straight lines.

Fabulous Food Festival
French Food Festival
Larose
(October)

CHAPTER 18

MISSISSIPPI
The Magnolia State

Capital: Jackson

Other Major Cities: Biloxi, Greenville

State Bird: Mockingbird

State Insect: Honeybee

State Tree: Magnolia

State Flower: Magnolia Blossom

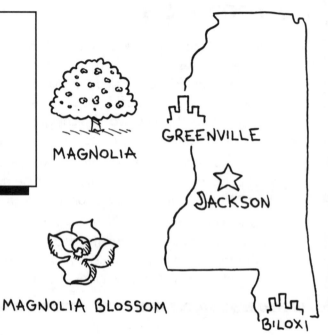

MAGNOLIA

MAGNOLIA BLOSSOM

GREENVILLE

JACKSON

BILOXI

Mississippi is a Native American word that means "big river." The first residents were Native Americans, including the Choctaw. The Mississippi Valley was part of the land claimed for France in 1682 by French explorer La Salle and named Louisiana after King Louis XIV. Both French and English settled in the area. England took control from the French, but lost Mississippi to the United States after the Revolutionary War. Mississippi, at first a territory of the United States, became the twentieth state in 1817. Mississippi is nicknamed the Magnolia State for the tree with pretty white flowers that grows all over the state.

Mississippi Foods

Mississippi is first in the country at producing farm-raised catfish, and commercial fishing boats bring in shrimp, oysters, and red snapper from the Gulf of Mexico. Farmers grow pecans, sweet potatoes, peaches, and watermelons.

···· Mississippi Mud Pie ····

The Mississippi River has several nicknames, such as "Old Man River" and "Big Muddy." This pie got its name when a waitress at a Mississippi restaurant remarked that the melted chocolate pie "reminds me of that Mississippi mud." Now you can find many different recipes for mud pies, mud cakes, and even mud beverages!

Time
40 minutes, including 20 minutes to freeze

Tools
skillet

medium bowl

9-inch pie plate

knife

spatula

Makes
8 to 12 servings

Ingredients

1 quart coffee ice cream

⅓ cup butter

1½ cups finely crushed chocolate wafers (about 25)

1½ cups fudge sauce, refrigerated

Steps

1. Set the coffee ice cream out at room temperature for 30 minutes.

2. Set the skillet over low heat and melt the butter.

3. Let the butter cool a minute, then pour it into the bowl. Add the crushed wafers and mix well.

4. Press the chocolate wafer mixture into the bottom and up the sides of the pie plate.

5. Fill the pie shell with coffee ice cream. Smooth the top of the ice cream evenly with a knife. Put the pie into the freezer until the ice cream is firm, about 20 minutes.

6. Top with the fudge sauce and spread with the spatula.

7. Slice and serve.

FUN FOOD FACTS

- Catfish are fish without scales. Catfish were first caught in Mississippi's rivers, but these days they more often come from special "farms," where they are raised in artificial ponds.

- A common dish served with catfish is called "hush puppies." While fresh-caught fish were cleaned, rolled in cornmeal, and fried over a fire, some cornmeal was mixed with milk or water and fried in the same pan. These fried balls of cornmeal were called hush puppies because they were given to the dogs to keep them from whining to be fed during the fish fry.

Fabulous Food Festival
Seafood Festival
Biloxi
(September)

CHAPTER 19

NORTH CAROLINA
The Tar Heel State

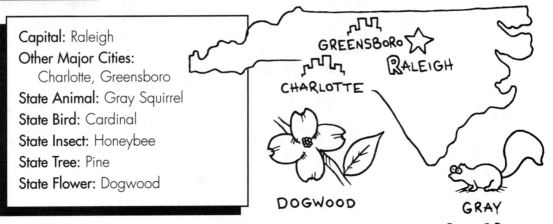

Capital: Raleigh
Other Major Cities:
 Charlotte, Greensboro
State Animal: Gray Squirrel
State Bird: Cardinal
State Insect: Honeybee
State Tree: Pine
State Flower: Dogwood

GREENSBORO
RALEIGH
CHARLOTTE
DOGWOOD
GRAY
SQUIRREL

In 1584, Sir Walter Raleigh sent explorers to the coast of what is now North Carolina to find a site for settlement. He established a settlement a year later on Roanoke Island, but the settlers soon packed up and returned to England. Raleigh persisted and sent another group of colonists to the same spot. After setting up the colony, Governor John White had to return to England. When he made it back to the settlement in 1589, he found that all of the colonists had disappeared. To this day, no one is sure what happened to them. They may have been killed off or absorbed into a Native American tribe.

When Europeans arrived, many Native American tribes, including the Cherokee, were living in what is now North Carolina. In 1629, Sir Robert Hatch gave the name Carolana to a piece of land given to him by King Charles I of England. The name comes from *Carolus,* the Latin word for Charles. The land stretched from Virginia to the Spanish colony of Florida. In 1663, King Charles II changed the name to Carolina and granted this territory to a number of wealthy friends. In 1712, Carolina was divided into North Carolina, South Carolina, and Georgia. North Carolina was one of the original thirteen colonies, and the first state to vote for independence.

It is unclear where the nickname the Tar Heel State came from. It may have been because North Carolina produced tar, but it was also said that North Carolina soldiers in the Civil War stuck to their posts like tar.

Time
2½ hours (you can cook the meat one day ahead)

Tools
large frying pan

cook's fork

heavy baking dish with lid

saucepan

oven mitts

Makes
6 servings

Barbecue (or BBQ) is very popular in North Carolina. BBQ in North Carolina means chopped pork cooked slowly over a hickory fire to take on the smoky flavor. But the key ingredient is the sauce. In eastern North Carolina, the BBQ has a vinegar-based sauce, while in western North Carolina, it has a tomato-based sauce. The recipe here is for the eastern version. BBQ is often served on a bun with sides such as coleslaw, hush puppies (fried cornmeal), and baked beans.

Ingredients

2 tablespoons oil

2 pound pork shoulder roast

½ cup ketchup

¼ cup apple cider vinegar

1 teaspoon garlic powder

½ teaspoon sugar

½ teaspoon salt

½ teaspoon cayenne pepper

cider vinegar as needed

hot sauce as needed

6 hamburger buns

Steps

1. Preheat oven to 300°F.

2. Heat the oil over medium heat in the frying pan. Add the pork roast and brown all sides, using the cook's fork to turn the meat (this takes about 3 to 5 minutes).

3. Using the fork, remove the meat from the frying pan and place it in the heavy baking dish.

4. In the saucepan, mix the ketchup, ¼ cup of vinegar, garlic powder, sugar, salt, and cayenne pepper. Bring to a boil over medium heat. Pour the sauce over the roast and cover the Dutch oven.

5. Bake for 2 hours. Spoon the sauce over the meat several times while it cooks. The meat is done when it is starting to separate from the bone. Remove the meat from the baking dish and let it cool for about 20 minutes.

6. When the meat has cooled, pull it into bite-sized pieces.
7. Season to taste with additional cider vinegar and hot sauce.
8. Serve on hamburger buns.

North Carolina Foods

North Carolina raises more turkeys than any other state, and is also well known for producing pork. Crops include peanuts and sweet potatoes.

FUN FOOD FACTS

- Rose Hill is said to be the home of the world's largest frying pan. The pan is 15 feet wide and is used to fry chicken during a town festival.

- The first Pepsi was served in 1895 in New Bern. It was created by Caleb Bradham, a New Bern pharmacist.

Fabulous Food Festival

Ham & Yam Festival
Smithfield
(April)

CHAPTER 20

SOUTH CAROLINA
The Palmetto State

Capital: Columbia
Other Major Cities: Charleston, Greenville
State Animal: White-tailed Deer
State Bird: Carolina Wren
State Insect: Carolina Mantis
State Tree: Palmetto
State Flower: Carolina Jessamine

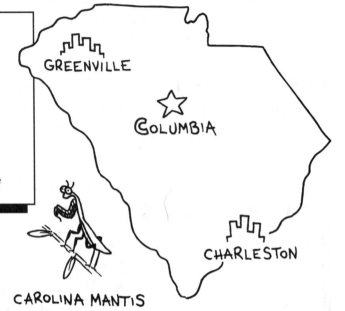

CAROLINA JESSAMINE   CAROLINA MANTIS

Like North Carolina, South Carolina was named for King Charles I of England. In 1663, King Charles II asked eight English noblemen, called lord proprietors, to send settlers to America and run settlements in the region between Virginia and Florida. The first settlers arrived in South Carolina in 1670 and eventually established what is now Charleston. In 1712, the region was divided into North Carolina, South Carolina, and Georgia. South Carolina was one of the original thirteen colonies, and became the eighth state in 1788.

South Carolina is called the Palmetto State because the palmetto, a kind of palm tree, is plentiful in the area. It may have earned this nickname during the Revolutionary War when South Carolina patriots destroyed a British warship from a small fort made of palmetto logs.

South Carolina Foods

South Carolina's Piedmont region is a farming area. Peaches, corn, and other fruits and vegetables are grown in the fertile land. Livestock raised include beef cattle, chickens, and hogs.

Peach Roll

South Carolina is the country's leading producer of peaches for the fresh market. Here's a way to keep that great peachy taste in a snack you can munch on anytime.

Ingredients

vegetable oil cooking spray
1 ½ cups chopped fresh peaches
1 tablespoon lemon juice
¼ teaspoon nutmeg

Steps

1. Preheat the oven to 175°F.

2. Spray the cookie sheet with vegetable oil cooking spray.

3. Put the peaches, lemon juice, and nutmeg in the blender container and blend until smooth.

4. Measure 2 cups of the peach mixture.

5. Use the sandwich spreader or table knife to spread the fruit mixture thinly over the cookie sheet.

6. Bake with the oven door slightly open for about 3 hours. Every 30 minutes, use oven mitts to remove the sheet from the oven and check to see if the peach roll is dry enough to peel off the cookie sheet. If it is still wet after 3 hours, use a spatula to flip it over and return it to the oven for about 10 minutes more.

7. Take the cookie sheet out of the oven using oven mitts. Peel the peach roll from the cookie sheet and place it on the cutting board.

8. Cut the peach roll crosswise into strips with the paring knife. Roll up the strips and store in plastic bags.

Time
20 minutes to prepare
plus
3 hours to cook

Tools
cookie sheet

measuring cup

blender

sandwich spreader
or
table knife

oven mitts

spatula

cutting board

paring knife

resealable plastic
sandwich bags

Makes
10 fruit rolls

FUN FOOD FACTS

- In 1890, the first tea plantation in the United States was started near Charleston.

- The first money crop in South Carolina was rice, which was grown for sale as early as the 1680s. Rice grew well in the swampy coastal areas. In Georgetown, there is a Rice Museum where you can learn all about the grain.

- A traditional South Carolina coastal stew with African origins is called Frogmore Stew, but it doesn't include any frogs. Its ingredients are seafood, sausage, and corn. Its name derives from a small town called Frogmore.

Fabulous Food Festival

Oyster Festival
Charleston
(February)

CHAPTER 21

TENNESSEE
The Volunteer State

Capital: Nashville

Other Major Cities: Knoxville, Memphis

State Animal: Raccoon

State Bird: Mockingbird

State Insects: Firefly, Ladybug

State Tree: Tulip Poplar

State Flower: Iris

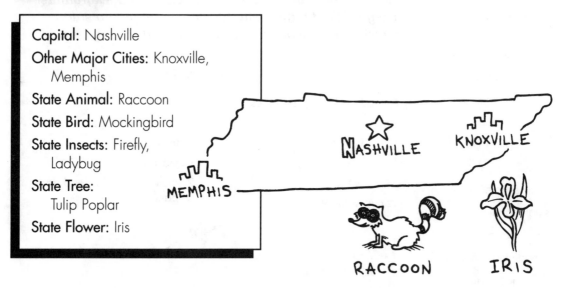

The first European settlers in Tennessee were British colonists from Virginia. Before the Revolutionary War, eastern Tennessee had a number of different governments. During the Revolutionary War, Tennesseans fought against the Cherokee, who sided with the British. At the end of the war, North Carolina claimed Tennessee, but it later became part of the "Territory of the U.S. South of the River Ohio." In 1796 Tennessee became the sixteenth state of the Union, the first to be created from a U.S. territory. The state took the name of a Cherokee village called Tanasie, or Tennessee. During the War of 1812 and the Mexican War, so many Tennesseans volunteered to fight that Tennessee earned the nickname the Volunteer State.

Tennessee Foods

Tennessee is well known for raising hogs and cattle. Poultry and milk are also important, as are crops such as tomatoes and apples.

···· German Potato Salad ····

Time
45 to 50 minutes

Tools
cooking fork

large stockpot

slotted spoon

colander

cutting board

peeler

serrated knife

small nonstick frying pan

paper towel

medium serving bowl

2-quart saucepan

Makes
8 servings

Many settlers in Tennessee had German backgrounds. They brought with them this version of potato salad, which uses a vinegar dressing instead of mayonnaise.

Ingredients

6 medium boiling potatoes

water

1 medium onion

1 stalk celery

3 slices bacon

½ cup white vinegar

½ cup water

1 tablespoon sugar

1 teaspoon salt

⅛ teaspoon pepper

2 tablespoons chopped fresh parsley

Steps

1. Wash and dry the potatoes. Prick each one several times with the fork.

2. Fill the stockpot ⅔ full of water to cook the potatoes. Bring the water to a boil. Use the slotted spoon to add the potatoes to the water and cook until they are tender when pierced with a fork. Drain the potatoes into a colander and run cold water on them for 1 minute.

3. Place the potatoes on the cutting board. Peel the potatoes, then slice them with the serrated knife into ¼-inch slices.

4. Remove the papery skin from the onion. Cut the onion in half and lay the halves flat-side down on the cutting board. Chop the onion into small pieces.

5. Wash the celery stalk and pat it dry. Slice the celery into ¼-inch slices.

6. Preheat the frying pan by placing it on medium heat for 2 minutes. Add the bacon and fry it until crisp. Add the onion and sauté for 2 minutes until it is tender. Remove the bacon and onion from the pan. Place the bacon on a paper towel to remove some of the fat.

7. Once it is cool, crush the bacon into small pieces.

8. In a medium serving bowl, toss together the potato slices, onion, celery, and bacon.

9. Put the vinegar, water, sugar, salt, and pepper in the saucepan. Stir and bring the mixture to a boil. Pour the mixture over the potatoes and toss gently. Sprinkle the parsley on top and serve.

Fabulous Food Festival

East Tennessee Strawberry Festival
Dayton (May)

FUN FOOD FACTS

- The world's first supermarket, Piggly Wiggly, was created by Clarence Saunders of Memphis.

- Tennessee hams, called "country hams," are quite different from Virginia's hams because Tennessee hogs are fed corn and other grains instead of peanuts. Ham with red-eye gravy is a traditional Tennessee dish. The gravy is called red-eye gravy because it includes pieces of fried ham that look like red eyes.

- In 1932, Herman Lay started a business in Nashville selling potato chips. Six years later he bought the company that supplied him with the potato chips and named it H. W. Lay & Company. Lay's potato chips merged with the Frito Company in 1961 to become Frito-Lay Inc.

CHAPTER 22

VIRGINIA
The Old Dominion

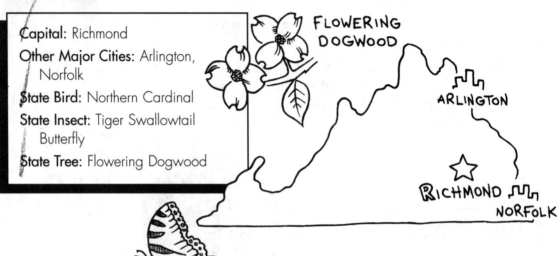

Capital: Richmond

Other Major Cities: Arlington, Norfolk

State Bird: Northern Cardinal

State Insect: Tiger Swallowtail Butterfly

State Tree: Flowering Dogwood

FLOWERING DOGWOOD

ARLINGTON

RICHMOND

NORFOLK

TIGER SWALLOWTAIL BUTTERFLY

In 1584, Queen Elizabeth I of England asked Sir Walter Raleigh to establish colonies in America. Although no permanent colonies were ever established by Raleigh, the eastern seaboard was named Virginia after Elizabeth, who was known as the Virgin Queen. In 1606, King James I chartered the Virginia Company of London to set up colonies in Virginia. Members of the Virginia Company built Jamestown, the first permanent English settlement in America. In 1624, the king of England took Virginia back from the Virginia Company and made it a colony. For Virginia's loyalty to England during the English Civil War in the mid-1600s, King Charles II made Virginia a dominion. He called Virginia his "Old Dominion" and this is how it got its nickname.

Virginia Foods

Farmers raise beef cattle, chickens, and turkeys. Crops include potatoes, sweet potatoes, peanuts, and apples. Commercial fishing boats off of the Atlantic coast bring in mainly oysters and crabs.

Virginia Ham with Cherry Sauce

Virginia is famous for its ham. Virginia ham gets its special flavor from the peanuts that are fed to the hogs as well as from how the hams are prepared. The hams are first allowed to absorb salt (this is called "curing"), and then placed over fires of hickory or oak wood to absorb the woodsmoke flavor (this is called "smoking"). Finally the hams are rubbed with pepper and hung to age for at least six months (this is called "aging").

Time
30 minutes

Tools
aluminum foil
medium saucepan
wooden spoon
oven mitts

Makes
4 servings

Ingredients

¾ pound boneless, cooked Virginia ham, sliced

3 tablespoons brown sugar

4 teaspoons cornstarch

¼ teaspoon cinnamon

1 cup apple juice

1 tablespoon vinegar

1 16-ounce can pitted tart red cherries packed in water, drained

Steps

1. Preheat the oven to 350°F.

2. Wrap the ham in foil. Place in the oven to heat up for 30 minutes.

3. While the ham is heating up, get the ingredients ready to make the cherry sauce.

4. About 10 minutes before the ham is warmed up, make the sauce. In the saucepan, mix together the brown sugar, cornstarch, and cinnamon. Stir in the apple juice and vinegar. Cook, stirring frequently, over medium heat until the sauce is thick and bubbly.

5. Cook the sauce 2 more minutes. Stir in the cherries. Cook for 4 more minutes or until the cherries are heated through.

6. Remove the foil-wrapped ham from the oven, using oven mitts. Place the ham on plates and ladle sauce over the ham.

FUN FOOD FACTS

- Thomas Jefferson, a Virginia native, is sometimes described as America's first gourmet. Until Thomas Jefferson bit into a tomato and decided it was edible and tasty, many people thought the tomato was poisonous. Thomas Jefferson is also credited with bringing pasta to America because he returned from one trip to Italy with a macaroni machine.

- Queen Victoria of England was so fond of the hams made in Virginia that she had a standing order for six Virginia hams each week.

- The earliest recipe for tomato ketchup comes from *The Virginia Housewife*, a cookbook from 1824. That first recipe included tomatoes, vinegar, and mushrooms or walnuts. Nowadays, we leave out the mushrooms and walnuts.

Fabulous Food Festival
Oyster Festival
Urbanna
(November)

CHAPTER 23

WEST VIRGINIA
The Mountain State

Capital: Charleston

Other Major Cities: Huntington, Wheeling

State Bird: Cardinal

State Tree: Sugar Maple

State Flower: Rhododendron

SUGAR MAPLE

RHODODENDRON

Traders from the Virginia Colony, the first permanent English settlement, ventured into eastern West Virginia in 1671 and claimed the land for England. The French also tried to claim this land. By the end of the French and Indian War in 1763, Great Britain had gained control of much of the land between the Atlantic Ocean and the Mississippi River, including West Virginia. West Virginia was considered a part of Virginia until the Civil War, when West Virginians refused to fight for the South. In 1863, West Virginia became the thirty-fifth state. West Virginia's nickname, the Mountain State, comes from the Appalachian Mountains.

West Virginia Foods

Farms produce beef and dairy cattle, chickens, and turkeys. Crops include apples, peaches, and corn.

···· Golden Delicious ···· Apple Pie

Time
30 minutes to prepare plus
45 to 55 minutes to bake

Tools
2 medium bowls

pastry blender

fork

rolling pin

9-inch pie pan

peeler

apple corer

knife

large bowl

cutting board

oven mitts

aluminum foil

Makes
1 9-inch pie, about 8 servings

Each fall, the town of Clay hosts a Golden Delicious Festival. Here's a recipe for a truly Delicious apple pie!

Ingredients

1¼ cups all-purpose flour

¼ teaspoon salt

⅓ cup vegetable shortening

3 to 4 tablespoons cold water

6 to 7 medium Golden Delicious apples

¼ cup sugar

2 tablespoons all-purpose flour

½ teaspoon cinnamon

¼ teaspoon ground ginger

1 teaspoon vanilla

2 tablespoons margarine

½ cup all-purpose flour

½ cup packed brown sugar

Steps

1. To make the pie crust, stir together 1¼ cups flour and the salt in a medium bowl.

2. Mix the shortening into the flour mixture with the pastry blender, using a back-and-forth motion, until the mixture looks like small peas.

3. Sprinkle 1 tablespoon of the water over part of the mixture. Gently toss with a fork. Add one more tablespoon of water and toss again. Repeat one more time.

4. Use your hands to form the dough into a ball. If it keeps falling apart, add ½ tablespoon of water.

5. Flatten the dough with your hands on a lightly floured surface. Use the rolling pin to roll out the dough. Always roll from the center to the edges. Form a circle of dough that is about 12 inches across.

6. Roll the dough onto the rolling pin, then unroll the dough over the pie pan. Use your hands to press the dough in place. Trim the pastry so it does not stick out over the edge of the pie pan.

7. Preheat the oven to 375°F.

8. To make the pie filling, first wash and dry the apples. Peel the apples.

9. Use the apple corer to core the apples. Slice the apples into ¼-inch slices.

10. In the large bowl, combine the sugar, 2 tablespoons flour, cinnamon, and ginger. Stir in the apples and vanilla.

11. Put the filling into the pie crust.

12. To make the crumb topping, first mix the ½ cup of flour and the brown sugar in the other medium bowl. Use the pastry blender to cut the margarine into the flour and brown sugar until the mixture looks like small peas.

13. Sprinkle the topping over the pie.

14. Bake the pie in the preheated oven for 25 minutes. Using oven mitts, loosely place a piece of aluminum foil over the edges of the pie so they don't get too brown. Bake 20 more minutes or until the top is golden and the fruit is bubbly.

FUN FOOD FACTS

- In 1753, a flood along the Potomac River covered the banks near Harper's Ferry with water and pumpkins. Since that time, local residents have made a tradition of using pumpkins to make pies and other dishes.

- The first Golden Delicious apples were grown from a seedling that grew up by chance on a West Virginia farm in 1890. By 1912, farmers were raising lots of beautiful Golden Delicious apples in West Virginia orchards.

Fabulous Food Festival

Black Walnut Festival
Spencer
(October)

THE MIDWEST

ILLINOIS
The Prairie State

CHAPTER 24

Capital: Springfield
Other Major Cities: Chicago, Rockford
State Animal: White-tailed Deer
State Bird: Cardinal
State Insect: Monarch Butterfly
State Tree: White Oak
State Flower: Violet

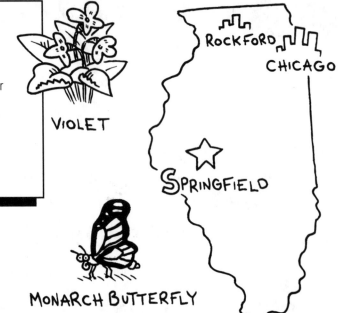

VIOLET

MONARCH BUTTERFLY

ROCKFORD
CHICAGO
SPRINGFIELD

Illinois got its name from a group of Native Americans called the Iliniwek, meaning "the people." The French trappers who first came to the area used the "ois" ending and called the river where most Iliniwek lived the Illinois. The first permanent settlers in Illinois were the French, who arrived in 1700. After losing the French and Indian War in 1763, France gave the land to England. In 1778, George Rogers Clark took over the settlements in Illinois and claimed them for Virginia. In 1809 the Illinois Territory was created, and in 1818 Illinois became the twenty-first state. Illinois is nicknamed the Prairie State because of its flat grasslands.

Illinois Foods

Thanks to fertile soil and lots of rain, Illinois grows many crops, among them corn, wheat, asparagus, pumpkins, and apples. Much livestock is raised, such as beef cattle and hogs.

Deep-Dish Pizza

Deep-dish pizza was first made at the Pizzeria Uno restaurant in Chicago in 1943. Because it's baked in a deep dish, it can hold more toppings than a regular pizza.

Ingredients

2 teaspoons shortening

1 package active dry yeast

1 cup lukewarm water

1 teaspoon sugar

1 teaspoon salt

2 tablespoons vegetable oil

2½ cups all-purpose flour

1 15½-ounce jar pizza sauce

6 ounces shredded mozzarella cheese

4 ounces sliced pepperoni or sliced cooked sausage

Steps

1. Preheat the oven to 425°F. Using the paper towel, grease the baking pan with the shortening.

2. Dissolve the yeast in lukewarm water in the bowl.

3. Stir in the sugar, salt, vegetable oil, and flour. Beat vigorously for 20 strokes.

4. Take the dough out of the bowl with your hands and place it on a lightly floured surface. If the dough is still sticky, add a small amount of flour to it.

5. Knead the dough for 3 minutes by flattening the dough into a circle, then picking up half the dough and pressing it down onto the other dough half. Give the dough a quarter turn and repeat.

6. Press the dough evenly on the bottom and halfway up the sides of the greased baking pan.

7. Spread the pizza sauce on the dough. Sprinkle on the shredded cheese and then the pepperoni or sausage.

8. Bake for 20 to 25 minutes or until the crust is lightly browned and the cheese is melted.

Time
20 minutes to prepare
plus
20 to 25 minutes
to bake

Tools
paper towel

9 x 13 x 2-inch baking pan

large bowl

spoon

oven mitts

Makes
12 servings

FUN FOOD FACTS

- Ray Kroc convinced the McDonald brothers, the owners of a restaurant in California, to let him open up branches of their restaurant in Illinois. Kroc opened the first new McDonald's in Des Plaines, and that was the beginning of the McDonald's chain. The original structure has since been torn down, but a replica containing a McDonald's museum now stands at that location.

- Sixty percent of the world's supply of horseradish comes from Illinois. Horseradish, originally from Europe, is the root of a plant in the mustard family. Its flavor is hot and sharp.

- The processed food companies Swift Premium, Oscar Mayer, Louis Rich, and Kraft were started in Illinois.

Fabulous Food Festival
Grape Festival
Nauvoo
(September)

CHAPTER 25

INDIANA
The Hoosier State

Capital: Indianapolis

Other Major Cities: Evansville, Fort Wayne

State Bird: Cardinal

State Tree: Tulip Tree

State Flower: Peony

TULIP TREE

PEONY

FORT WAYNE

INDIANAPOLIS

EVANSVILLE

Indiana means "land of the Indians." When the first white explorers arrived in what is now known as Indiana, they found a tribe of Native Americans called the Miamis. In 1732, French fur traders were the first to build a permanent settlement. Later, in 1763, France gave Britain its claims to Indiana and other regions after France lost the French and Indian War. During the Revolutionary War, the colonists took control of the northwest area, which included Indiana, from the English. Indiana became part of the Northwest Territory in 1787 and then became the Indiana Territory in 1799. Indiana was admitted as the nineteenth state in 1816.

For over 150 years the people of Indiana have been called Hoosiers. No one knows exactly how Indiana got this nickname, but it has been used since the 1830s.

Indiana Foods

Indiana is a leading state in egg production. It also produces more corn for popcorn than any other state, and it supplies much of the country's peppermint and spearmint. Other crops include wheat, potatoes, and apples. Farms also produce hogs and chickens.

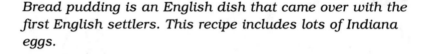

Bread Pudding

Time
10 minutes to prepare
plus
35 to 45 minutes
to bake

Tools
paper towel

2-quart baking dish

electric mixer

medium bowl

oven mitts

Makes
4 servings

Bread pudding is an English dish that came over with the first English settlers. This recipe includes lots of Indiana eggs.

Ingredients

2 teaspoons shortening

3 cups day-old bread, cubed (about 5 slices)

½ cup raisins

4 eggs

2 cups milk

⅓ cup sugar

1 teaspoon vanilla

ice cream, optional

Steps

1. Preheat the oven to 350°F. Using the paper towel, grease the baking dish with the shortening.

2. Put the bread cubes and raisins in the baking dish and toss to mix.

3. In the bowl, beat together the eggs, milk, sugar, and vanilla with the electric mixer. Pour the mixture over the bread cubes and raisins.

4. Bake for 35 to 45 minutes or until a knife inserted in the middle comes out clean. Serve warm or chilled with ice cream.

FUN FOOD FACTS

- Indiana chickens lay 5 billion eggs each year. That's one for everyone in the world! On the first weekend of June, the town of Mentone holds an Egg Festival.

- Indiana is the home of Orville Redenbacher, the king of popcorn. He worked for over twenty years at Purdue University to perfect a light and fluffy popcorn. At the annual Popcorn Festival in Valparaiso, you can enjoy popcorn kernel races, popcorn dances, and many popcorn treats, such as popcorn lollipops!

Fabulous Food Festival
Festival of Gingerbread
Fort Wayne
(November/ December)

CHAPTER 26

IOWA
The Hawkeye State

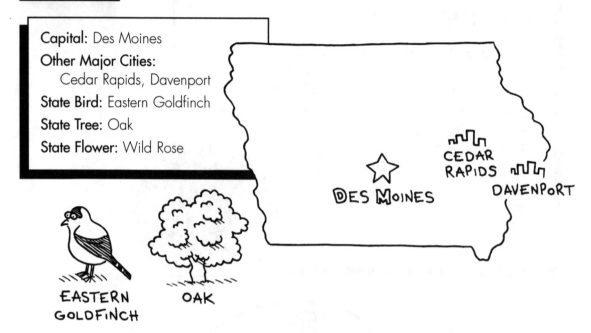

Capital: Des Moines
Other Major Cities:
   Cedar Rapids, Davenport
State Bird: Eastern Goldfinch
State Tree: Oak
State Flower: Wild Rose

DES MOINES

CEDAR RAPIDS

DAVENPORT

EASTERN GOLDFINCH

OAK

Iowa takes its name from a tribe of Native Americans who lived in the area when the earliest settlers arrived. Their word *iowa* was thought to mean "beautiful land." In 1682, the French explorer La Salle claimed the Mississippi Valley for France and named it Louisiana after King Louis XIV. This land included Iowa. When France sold the Louisiana Territory in 1803 to the United States, there were almost no settlers in the region that became Iowa. Iowa was officially closed to settlement until 1832 because it was being used to relocate the Sauk and Fox tribes from Illinois. When these tribes were defeated in the Black Hawk War in 1832, a section of Iowa along the Mississippi River was opened for settlement. Eventually, Iowa's rich farmland attracted people from other states and from Europe. The Territory of Iowa, which included parts of other states, was created in 1838, and in 1846 present-day Iowa was carved out of the territory and became the twenty-ninth state. Iowa is called the Hawkeye State to honor Chief Black Hawk, a famous Sauk leader.

Corn Dogs

Iowa's most famous crop is corn. Here's a fun way to wrap a hot dog!

Ingredients

1 cup all-purpose flour	2 tablespoons margarine, cold
1 teaspoon sugar	¾ cup milk
½ teaspoon salt	1 large egg
1 teaspoon baking powder	8 hot dogs
1 dash cayenne pepper	2 tablespoons vegetable oil
⅔ cup cornmeal	mustard

Steps

1. In the medium bowl, use the sifter to sift together the flour, sugar, salt, baking powder, and pepper. Stir in the cornmeal.

2. Cut the margarine into small pieces with a knife. Cut the margarine into the flour mixture by rocking the pastry blender back and forth until the mixture resembles small peas.

3. Whisk the milk and the egg together in the small bowl.

4. Pour the milk mixture into the flour mixture and stir with the wooden spoon until the batter is well blended. The batter will be thick.

5. Using the sandwich spreader, spread each hot dog with the batter until it is evenly coated.

6. Put the oil in a large sauté pan and warm up over medium heat.

7. Line the plate with paper towels.

8. Fry the hot dogs for 2 to 4 minutes on each side until golden brown. Turn with the fork to brown them on all sides.

9. Use the tongs to remove the cooked hot dogs to the plate and allow them to drain for several minutes.

Time
20 to 25 minutes

Tools
medium bowl
sifter
knife
pastry blender
wire whip
small bowl
wooden spoon
sandwich spreader
large sauté pan
plate
paper towels
fork
tongs
10 bamboo skewers

Makes
8 servings

10. Insert a bamboo skewer into one end of each hot dog and eat like an ice cream pop. Serve with mustard.

Iowa Foods

Iowa has excellent farmland and lots of it! Iowa is well known for producing corn, apples, hogs, beef, turkey, and chickens.

FUN FOOD FACTS

- The Red Delicious apple was developed at an orchard near East Peru in the 1880s. It was first called a Hawkeye apple. The Stark Brothers Nursery bought the rights to this new apple variety and called it a Delicious apple.

- On summer nights, Iowa farmers say you can hear the corn growing. During peak growing time, corn stalks can actually grow 3 to 5 inches a day.

Fabulous Food Festival
Strawberry Days
Strawberry Point
(June)

KANSAS
Midway, U.S.A.

CHAPTER 27

Capital: Topeka

Other Major Cities: Kansas City,
  Wichita

State Bird: Western Meadowlark

State Tree: Cottonwood

State Flower: Sunflower

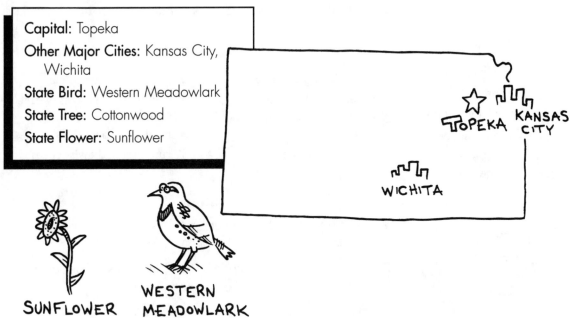

SUNFLOWER   WESTERN
               MEADOWLARK

Kansas was named after a Native American group called the Kansa, meaning "people of the south wind." In 1682, the area we now know as Kansas was part of the territory claimed by French explorer La Salle and named Louisiana after King Louis XIV. Along with the rest of the territory, it was bought by the United States in 1803 as part of the Louisiana Purchase. Later, trails taking settlers out West went though parts of Kansas. In 1854 the Kansas Territory was created. In 1861, Kansas became the thirty-fourth state. Kansas is called Midway, U.S.A. because it is right in the middle of the United States.

Kansas Foods

Kansas is first in the country in producing wheat. Other crops include corn, sugar beets, oats, and apples. Livestock is also important, and Kansas is a leading producer of beef cattle.

Grilled Swiss Cheeseburger with Sliced Mushrooms

Time
20 to 25 minutes

Tools
medium mixing bowl

broiling pan

oven mitts

nonstick frying pan

wooden spoon

Makes
4 large burgers

Kansas is well known for its quality beef cattle. Use some high-quality beef to make this gourmet hamburger!

Ingredients

1 pound lean ground beef

2 tablespoons ketchup

2 tablespoons Worcestershire sauce

½ teaspoon salt

dash pepper

2 tablespoons margarine

1 cup fresh mushrooms, washed and sliced

4 hamburger buns, split

¾ cup shredded Swiss cheese

Steps

1. Stir the beef, ketchup, Worcestershire sauce, salt, and pepper together in the bowl. Mix well with your hands.

2. Shape the meat mixture into four 1-inch-thick burger patties and put them on the broiling pan.

3. Preheat the broiler. Place the broiling pan about 4 to 5 inches from the heat element or flame. Broil about 8 minutes on each side until no pink meat remains.

4. Using oven mitts, remove the pan from the oven. Allow the burgers to rest for about 10 minutes. Turn the broiler off.

5. Meanwhile, preheat the frying pan on medium heat. Put the margarine in the pan. Sauté the mushrooms for about 3 to 4 minutes or until cooked through.

6. Turn the broiler on again. Assemble the cooked burgers on another broiling pan by placing a burger on the bottom half of each bun. Top each burger with shredded cheese and mushrooms. Lay the top halves of the buns upside down on the broiling pan.

7. Broil the assembled burgers and top halves of the buns just until the cheese melts and the rolls are lightly toasted.

FUN FOOD FACTS

- When the Mennonites, a religious group, came to Kansas in the 1870s from Russia, they found the wheat farmers almost starving. Each Mennonite family had brought seeds of the wheat they had grown in Russia. Their wheat crops flourished and made wheat growing possible again.

- The first big food service chain in the United States, Harvey House, started with a restaurant in Topeka in 1876. Fred Harvey's restaurants were the first to offer quality meals in a civilized atmosphere to passengers of the Santa Fe Railroad. When Harvey had problems with male waiters drinking and brawling, he decided to try to get women to work for him instead. The waitresses he hired from the East became known as the Harvey Girls and they received much credit for civilizing the West. Many eventually married and settled down in the areas where they worked.

- The first Pizza Hut restaurant opened in Kansas in 1958.

Fabulous Food Festival
International Pancake Race
Liberal
(February)

MICHIGAN
The Wolverine State

Capital: Lansing

Other Major Cities: Detroit, Grand Rapids

State Animal: Painted Turtle

State Bird: Robin

State Tree: White Pine

State Flower: Apple Blossom

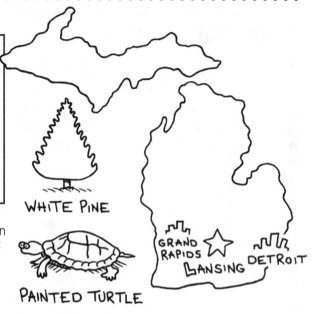

WHITE PINE

PAINTED TURTLE

GRAND RAPIDS
LANSING
DETROIT

The state of Michigan is named for one of the lakes it borders, Lake Michigan. The name Michigan originally came from the Algonquin Indian word *michigama,* meaning "great lake." Michigan was first controlled by the French, and then by the English. After the Revolutionary War it became part of the Northwest Territory of the United States. In 1805, the Michigan Territory was carved out of the Northwest Territory. When public lands in Michigan became available for purchase in 1818, and again when the Erie Canal was opened in 1925, many more settlers came. In 1837, Michigan was admitted as the twenty-sixth state. Because Michigan fur traders traded wolverine furs during the 1600s and 1700s, the state is known as the Wolverine State. A wolverine is an animal native to northern North America that looks something like a small bear.

Michigan Foods

The farms on Michigan's Lower Peninsula grow many foods. Michigan is first in the country in producing tart cherries and dry beans. Tart cherries are mainly used to make cherry pie filling. Michigan's cherry orchards are located along Lake Michigan, where the lake tempers the weather and the soil and elevation are just right for ideal growing.

Ice Cream with Cherry Sauce in a Tortilla Shell

Here's a delicious way to use those Michigan cherries!

Ingredients

1 16-ounce can cherry pie filling

1 teaspoon almond extract

1 teaspoon cinnamon

1 teaspoon sugar

4 tortilla shells, shaped like bowls

1 pint vanilla ice cream

Time
10 minutes

Tools
small saucepan

Makes
4 servings

Steps

1. In the saucepan, heat up the pie filling and almond extract.

2. Sprinkle the cinnamon and sugar over the tortilla shells.

3. Fill each shell with 2 scoops of ice cream.

4. Top with warm cherry pie filling and serve immediately.

FUN FOOD FACTS

- Mining families from Cornwall, a part of England, brought a recipe for "pasties" with them when they settled in Michigan during the mid-1800s. Pasties look like half moons and are made of pastry dough curled around a filling and baked. They are filled with chopped beef, vegetables, and gravy, cream, or butter. Pasties became a portable meal for the miners in Michigan during the 1800s. Pasties are still eaten in Michigan and May 24 is Pasty Day.

- In the late 1800s, John Harvey Kellogg, who managed the Battle Creek Sanitarium, invented wheat flakes in a search for healthier breakfast foods. C. W. Post soon invented what became Grape Nuts, and Kellogg's brother Will invented cornflakes. These first breakfast cereals were a huge success. Kellogg's is still based in Battle Creek.

- In 1987, a Traverse City bakery made the biggest cherry pie ever. It was over 17 feet wide and weighed more than 14 tons!

Fabulous Food **Festival**
Cereal Festival
Battle Creek
(June)

CHAPTER 29

INNESOTA
The Land of 10,000 Lakes

Capital: St. Paul

Other Major Cities: Bloomington, Minneapolis

State Bird: Common Loon

State Tree: Norway Pine

State Flower: Showy Lady's Slipper

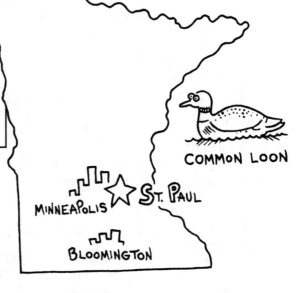

COMMON LOON

MINNEAPOLIS ST. PAUL

BLOOMINGTON

SHOWY
LADY'S SLIPPER

The word *minisota* means "sky-tinted water" in the Dakota Sioux language. The first Europeans to visit Minnesota were probably French fur traders during the 1650s. They traded with the Santee Sioux and other Native American groups. At the end of the French and Indian War in 1763, France had to give all of its land in Canada and east of the Mississippi, including northern and eastern Minnesota, to England. Spain received all of its land west of the Mississippi, including western Minnesota. After the Revolutionary War, England gave eastern Minnesota, but not northern Minnesota, to the new United States of America. Western Minnesota was sold back to the United States as part of the Louisiana Purchase in 1803, and Britain was forced to give up northern Minnesota after the War of 1812. The Minnesota Territory was created in 1849, and two years later the United States pushed many Native Americans onto reservations to make room for more white settlers. Minnesota was admitted as the thirty-second state in 1858. Minnesota has lots of water. Over 10,000 lakes dot the landscape, giving the state its nickname, the Land of 10,000 Lakes.

Time
30 minutes

Tools
small bowl

fork

large bowl

wooden spoon

shallow dish

large sauté pan with cover

large saucepan

colander

Makes
6 servings

Many Swedish immigrants and other Scandinavians settled in Minnesota. They introduced this distinctive way of preparing meatballs.

Ingredients

1 large egg
1 pound lean ground beef
½ pound ground pork
½ cup leftover mashed potatoes
1 cup bread crumbs
1 teaspoon salt

1 teaspoon brown sugar
½ teaspoon pepper
½ teaspoon allspice
½ teaspoon ground nutmeg
2 tablespoons vegetable oil
1 cup dry noodles

Steps

1. In the small bowl, beat the egg with the fork.

2. Put the ground beef, ground pork, mashed potatoes, ½ cup bread crumbs, salt, brown sugar, pepper, allspice, and nutmeg in the large bowl. Add the beaten egg and mix well with the wooden spoon.

3. Shape the mixture into 20 meatballs.

4. Put ½ cup bread crumbs in the shallow dish. Roll the meatballs in the bread crumbs to coat them.

5. Put the oil in the large sauté pan and heat over medium heat.

6. Add the meatballs to the pan and brown on all sides, turning them with the wooden spoon.

7. Reduce heat, cover, and cook about 15 minutes.

8. While the meatballs cook, prepare the noodles in the saucepan according to package instructions. Drain them in the colander.

9. Serve the meatballs over the noodles.

Minnesota Foods

Minnesota is first in the country in the production of sugar beets, and is also a major producer of milk and dairy products. Farmers grow sweet corn, wheat, and apples. Important livestock include beef cattle and hogs. Commercial fishing is a big industry and boats on Lake Superior bring in lake trout and other fish.

FUN FOOD FACTS

- Two major food companies got their start in Minneapolis: Pillsbury and Green Giant. Charles Pillsbury started his business with a flour mill. Green Giant started out by canning corn. Pillsbury now owns Green Giant.

- Minnesota is well known for its wild rice. Wild rice, the kernels of a grass that grows in shallow lakes, was first harvested by Native Americans. Native American groups, such as the Ojibwa, continue to use their canoes to harvest wild rice every August and September.

- Pancake syrup using maple syrup and cane sugar syrup was first invented by Patrick J. Towle, a St. Paul grocer who wanted to give people the flavor of maple syrup without the high price. He gave his syrup the name of Log Cabin to honor his boyhood hero, Abraham Lincoln.

Fabulous Food Festival
Taste of Minnesota Food Festival
St. Paul
(July)

CHAPTER 30

MISSOURI
The Show Me State

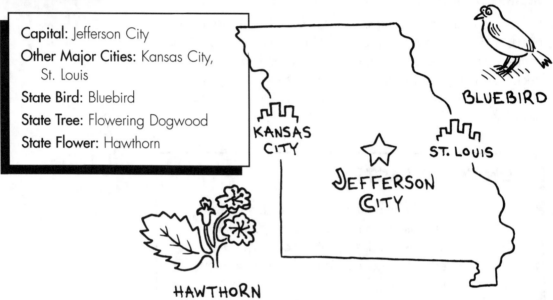

Capital: Jefferson City

Other Major Cities: Kansas City, St. Louis

State Bird: Bluebird

State Tree: Flowering Dogwood

State Flower: Hawthorn

BLUEBIRD

KANSAS CITY

JEFFERSON CITY

ST. LOUIS

HAWTHORN

Missouri is named after the Missouri Indians. Their name may have meant "people of the big canoe." The Missouri used their large dugout canoes on Missouri's many waterways, including the Missouri River and the Mississippi River. The first European settlers to this area were French trappers and fur traders who arrived in the late 1600s and set up trading posts on the rivers. In 1803, the United States bought the land that would become Missouri as part of the Louisiana Purchase. In 1812 part of the Louisiana Territory was renamed the Missouri Territory and in 1821 Missouri became the twenty-fourth state. Missouri came to be called the Show Me State after a Missouri Congressman said in a speech in 1899, " . . . frothy eloquence neither convinces nor satisfies me. I am from Missouri. You have got to show me."

Missouri Foods

Only Texas has more farms than Missouri. Missouri is known for producing beef cattle, hogs, and turkeys, as well as dairy products. Corn, apples, and black walnuts are some of the important crops.

Black Walnut Quickbread

Missouri is the biggest producer of black walnuts in the United States. Walnuts add a nice crunch to this easy quickbread.

Ingredients

vegetable oil cooking spray

3 cups all-purpose flour

5 teaspoons baking powder

½ cup sugar

1 teaspoon salt

1 teaspoon cinnamon

¼ teaspoon ground nutmeg

2 large eggs

1 cup milk

1 teaspoon vanilla extract

½ cup melted margarine

1 cup chopped black walnuts

Steps

1. Preheat the oven to 350°F. Spray the loaf pan with vegetable oil cooking spray.

2. In the large mixing bowl, sift together the flour, baking powder, sugar, salt, cinnamon, and nutmeg.

3. In the medium bowl, whisk together the eggs, milk, vanilla extract, and melted margarine.

4. Add the egg mixture to the flour mixture and stir with a wooden spoon just until the dry ingredients are moistened. Fold in the walnuts.

5. Pour the batter into the prepared pan. Bake for about 1 hour or until the center springs back when touched. Remove from the oven and cool on the wire rack for 10 minutes before removing from the pan.

Time
30 minutes to prepare
plus
60 minutes to bake

Tools
9 x 5 x 3-inch loaf pan

sifter

large mixing bowl

medium bowl

wire whip

wooden spoon

oven mitts

wire rack

Makes
1 loaf or 16 servings

FUN FOOD FACTS

- Peanut butter was first made in St. Louis by a physician who spread mashed peanuts on bread for his patients.
- Ice cream cones and hot dogs on buns were first introduced at the St. Louis World's Fair in 1904.
- Wild pecans are harvested by attaching a mechanical shaker to the tree. The shaker shakes the tree and down come the nuts.

Fabulous Food Festival

Ozark Ham and Turkey Festival
California, Missouri
(September)

CHAPTER 31

NEBRASKA
The Cornhusker State

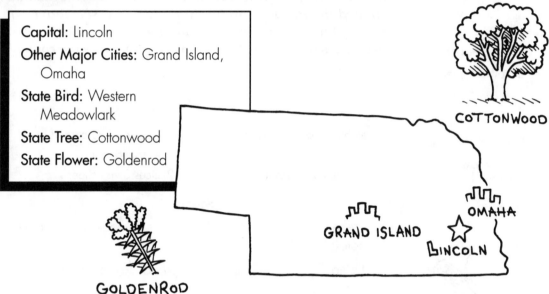

Capital: Lincoln

Other Major Cities: Grand Island, Omaha

State Bird: Western Meadowlark

State Tree: Cottonwood

State Flower: Goldenrod

COTTONWOOD

OMAHA

GRAND ISLAND

LINCOLN

GOLDENROD

Nebraska got its name from the Oto Indian word *nebrathka*, which means "flat water," and referred to what is now called the Platte River. When the United States bought the Louisiana Territory from France in 1803, Nebraska was a part of this land. Until 1854, white settlers were not allowed in Nebraska because it was reserved as Indian land. When the Nebraska Territory, including current-day Nebraska and parts of several other states, was created in 1854, settlers were allowed to come. In 1862, the Homestead Act encouraged even more settlers to come by offering free land. Nebraska became the thirty-seventh state in 1867. Nebraska's nickname, the Cornhusker State, comes from corn, the state's leading crop, and from cornhusking contests held in rural Nebraskan towns in the fall.

Nebraska Foods

Nebraska is well known for growing corn and raising beef cattle. Other crops include wheat, oats, and potatoes.

•••• Reuben Sandwich ••••

Time
15 minutes

Tools
broiler pan

sandwich spreader

oven mitts

knife

12 decorative toothpicks

Makes
6 sandwiches

In the 1920s, Reuben Kay, a wholesale grocer in Omaha, created the Reuben sandwich. He kept it a secret among a few of his friends, but one day the recipe leaked out because someone in Omaha entered it in a recipe contest and won!

Ingredients

vegetable oil cooking spray

12 slices rye bread

¾ cup Russian dressing

18 slices cooked corned beef

1 cup sauerkraut

12 slices Swiss cheese

Steps

1. Preheat the broiler. Spray the pan with vegetable oil cooking spray.

2. Using the sandwich spreader, spread 6 slices of bread with Russian dressing.

3. On each of the 6 bread slices, arrange the sandwich by placing 3 slices of corned beef, a heaping tablespoon of sauerkraut, and 2 slices of cheese. Place on the broiler pan.

4. Place the remaining 6 bread slices on the broiler pan to toast.

5. Place the pan under the broiler about 6 inches away from the heating element or flame. Wait until the cheese is melted and bread slices are lightly toasted. This takes about 2 minutes.

6. Cover the sandwiches. Cut in half. Put a decorative toothpick through each sandwich half to keep it together.

FUN FOOD FACTS

- The Coffee Burger at Sioux Sundries in Harriston makes what might be the world's largest hamburgers—28 ounces of beef!

- One of the largest food companies in the world, ConAgra, has its headquarters in Grand Island, where it started in business as the Nebraska Consolidated Mills in 1919. ConAgra is today widely diversified, including brands such as Healthy Choice and Armour.

Fabulous Food Festival
Wayne Chicken Show
Wayne
(July)

CHAPTER 32

NORTH DAKOTA
The Flickertail State

Capital: Bismarck

Other Major Cities: Fargo, Grand Forks

State Bird: Western Meadowlark

State Tree: American Elm

State Flower: Wild Prairie Rose

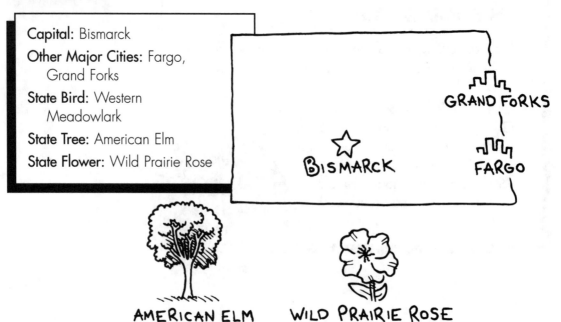

GRAND FORKS

BISMARCK

FARGO

AMERICAN ELM   WILD PRAIRIE ROSE

North Dakota was named after the Dakota Indians. *Dakota* means "friends." The Dakota were also called the Lakotas or Sioux. In 1861, the Dakota Territory was established. It included North and South Dakota as well as parts of Wyoming and Montana. Europeans did not settle in North Dakota until the 1870s. The territory was divided into North and South Dakota and the Dakotas became the thirty-ninth and fortieth states in 1889. North Dakota is called the Flickertail State because there are many flickertail ground squirrels in central North Dakota.

North Dakota Foods

North Dakota is first in the country in growing sunflower seeds and second in the country in growing wheat. Much livestock, such as beef cattle, is raised. Some North Dakota farmers are also beekeepers.

•••• Macaroni and Cheese ••••

Many farmers in North Dakota plant a special variety of wheat called durum wheat. Durum wheat is used to make macaroni, spaghetti, and other types of pasta.

Ingredients

vegetable oil cooking spray

water

½ pound elbow macaroni

2 tablespoons margarine

¼ cup all-purpose flour

2 cups milk

6 ounces shredded cheddar cheese

3 ounces shredded Swiss cheese

¼ teaspoon salt

½ cup toasted wheat germ

Steps

1. Preheat the oven to 350°F. Spray the baking dish with vegetable oil cooking spray.

2. Fill the 4-quart saucepan half full with water and bring to a boil over high heat. Add the macaroni. Cook for as long as it says on the box. When the macaroni is done, drain it in the colander, then put it back in the saucepan. Set aside.

3. In the 3-quart saucepan, melt the margarine on low heat. Whisk in the flour and continue to cook until the mixture is bubbly, about 3 minutes. Do not brown.

4. Slowly add the milk to the pan and stir with the wooden spoon over medium heat until the mixture thickens. Remove from the heat.

5. Add the cheddar cheese, Swiss cheese, and salt to the pot and stir again until all the cheese is melted.

6. Add the cheese sauce to the drained pasta and mix, coating the pasta well. Place the pasta in the prepared baking dish. Sprinkle with toasted wheat germ.

7. Bake for 25 to 30 minutes.

Time
20 minutes to prepare
plus
25 to 30 minutes to bake

Tools
1-quart baking dish

4-quart saucepan

colander

3-quart saucepan

wire whip

wooden spoon

oven mitts

Makes
4 servings

FUN FOOD FACTS

- The hot breakfast cereal Cream of Wheat was developed in Grand Forks in 1893. It was made by a mill employee from the part of the wheat grain that wasn't used to make flour.

- In 1988, the North and South Dakota Wheat Commissions developed a recipe for Dakota Bread to honor the one hundredth anniversary of their statehood. The bread uses grains grown in both states such as wheat, rye, and oats.

Fabulous Food Festival
Potato Bowl
Grand Forks
(September)

CHAPTER 33

OHIO
The Buckeye State

Capital: Columbus

Other Major Cities: Cincinnati, Cleveland

State Animal: White-tailed Deer

State Bird: Cardinal

State Insect: Ladybug

State Tree: Buckeye

State Flower: Scarlet Carnation

SCARLET CARNATION

BUCKEYE

Ohio got its name from the Ohio River, which the Iroquois Indians called *o-hy-o*, meaning "something large." Although the French were the first to claim the area, they never had a permanent settlement there. In 1763 France gave the land that included what is now Ohio to England. After the Revolutionary War, the land became part of the United States. In 1787, the Northwest Territory, which included Ohio, was created. By 1800, the Ohio Territory was separated from the Northwest Territory and only three years later, it became the seventeenth state. Ohio is called the Buckeye State because buckeye trees once grew on many of Ohio's hills and plains. The buckeye tree is a medium-size shade tree with large seeds that look like the eye of a buck, or male deer.

Ohio Foods

Ohio produces more hothouse tomatoes (meaning they are grown in a greenhouse) than any other state except California. Farmers also grow wheat, cucumbers, and apples.

·····Cincinnati Chili over Pasta·····

Time
70 minutes

Tools
cutting board

knife

large saucepan

wooden spoon

large stockpot

colander

Makes
6 servings

By the 1920s, chili was already established as a classic Texan dish, but Cincinnati also has a reputation for fine chili. Cooks in a Greek-owned restaurant adapted a Texas chili recipe by using traditional Mediterranean herbs and spices, such as oregano, cumin, and cloves, and serving the chili over pasta.

Ingredients

1 medium onion

2 stalks celery

2 cloves garlic

1 pound lean ground beef

1 cup tomato sauce

½ cup beef broth

1 tablespoon chili powder

2 tablespoons honey

1 teaspoon ground cumin

¼ teaspoon ground cloves

½ teaspoon oregano

1 15-ounce can kidney beans, drained

water

8 ounces thin spaghetti

1 cup shredded cheddar cheese

Steps

1. On the cutting board, remove the papery skin from the onion. Cut the onion in half. Lay the halves flat side down on the board and chop into small pieces.

2. Wash and dry the celery. Cut each stalk in half lengthwise, then cut into small pieces.

3. Peel and slice the garlic cloves.

4. Preheat the large saucepan on medium heat for 2 minutes.

5. Add the beef, onions, celery, and garlic to the pot and cook, stirring until the beef is brown and the vegetables are tender. Drain the fat from the pot.

6. Stir in the tomato sauce, beef broth, chili powder, honey, cumin, cloves, and oregano and bring the mixture to a boil. Lower the heat to simmer and cover. Cook for 30 minutes.

7. Add the kidney beans and cook 15 minutes more.

8. While the kidney beans are cooking in the chili, fill the stockpot two-thirds full with water and bring to a boil. Add the spaghetti and boil it according to package directions. When done, drain the spaghetti in the colander.

9. Divide the spaghetti among 6 soup bowls. Top with the chili and shredded cheese. Serve immediately.

FUN FOOD FACTS

- Many of the apple trees in Ohio were planted by the frontier hero nicknamed Johnny Appleseed. (His real name was John Chapman.) In the early 1800s he brought apple seeds from Massachusetts and planted them throughout Ohio and Indiana.

- Oatmeal became popular as a cereal when a mill near Akron started producing processed oatmeal. Until that time, oatmeal was fed to horses or given as a medicine.

- Ice cream on a stick was invented by the Burt family in Youngstown in 1920. This was the beginning of Good Humor Ice Cream.

Fabulous Food Festival
Cherry Festival
Bellevue
(June)

CHAPTER 34

SOUTH DAKOTA
The Land of Infinite Variety

Capital: Pierre

Other Major Cities: Sioux Falls, Rapid City

State Animal: Coyote

State Bird: Ring-necked Pheasant

State Insect: Honeybee

State Tree: Black Hills Spruce

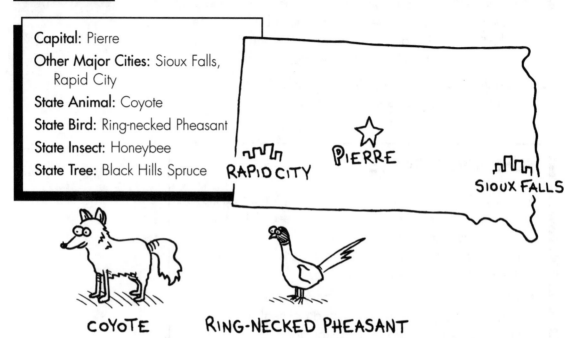

COYOTE   RING-NECKED PHEASANT

Like North Dakota, South Dakota was named after the Dakota Indians. *Dakota* means "friends." The United States bought what is now South Dakota from the French as part of the Louisiana Purchase in 1803. South Dakota was not settled until the middle and late 1800s. When gold was discovered in the Black Hills in 1874, many fortune hunters poured into the area. The territory was divided into North and South Dakota before the Dakotas became the thirty-ninth and fortieth states in 1889. South Dakota is nicknamed the Land of Infinite Variety because of its many different landforms, which include prairies, plains, mountains, and valleys. It is also called the Mount Rushmore State, because of the huge sculptures of George Washington, Thomas Jefferson, Theodore Roosevelt, and Abraham Lincoln carved into the side of Mount Rushmore in the 1920s.

South Dakota Foods

South Dakota is a major producer of beef cattle and hogs. Important crops include wheat, corn, and sunflower seeds.

Cornmeal Mush with Molasses

If you have ever read the Little House on the Prairie series by Laura Ingalls Wilder, you might remember that her family settled in De Smet, South Dakota, in 1879, after living in several other Midwestern states. Her family often ate cornmeal mush, as did many other pioneering families on the prairie, with molasses and cream when it was available.

Time
20 minutes

Tools
saucepan

small bowl

wooden spoon

Makes
6 servings

Ingredients

3 cups water

½ teaspoon salt

1 cup yellow cornmeal

1 cup cold water

molasses, as needed

light cream, as needed

Steps

1. Put the 3 cups of water and salt in the saucepan. Bring to a boil.

2. Mix the cornmeal with 1 cup of cold water in the small bowl. Add to the boiling water. Bring to a boil again, stirring constantly with the wooden spoon.

3. Reduce heat to low and cook 15 minutes. Stir often to get rid of lumps and prevent the mush from sticking to the pan.

4. Pour into cereal bowls. Serve with molasses and cream.

FUN FOOD FACTS

- In Mitchell you will find a tourist attraction called the Corn Palace. Its name comes from the colorful murals that cover its outer walls—they are made of corn! The building is decorated with bushels of corn, and nearby lampposts are decorated with corncobs.

- Just outside of the South Dakota region known as the Badlands, Ted and Dorothy Hustead bought a drug store in a town called Wall in 1931. They realized that if they advertised free ice water, they would attract lots of tourists who visit during the hot summer. Their idea was so successful that Wall Drug, which includes its own re-created western town, restaurant, and picnic area, now gets about 20,000 customers on a hot summer day.

Fabulous Food Festival
Schmeckfest
(German Food Festival)
Freeman
(March/April)

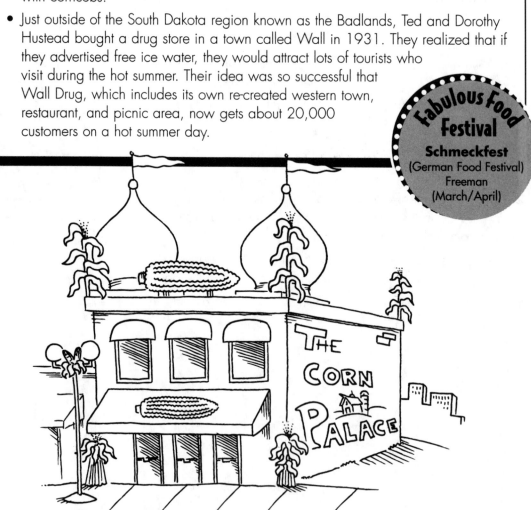

CHAPTER 35

WISCONSIN
America's Dairyland

Capital: Madison

Other Major Cities: Green Bay, Milwaukee

State Animal: Badger

State Bird: Robin

State Tree: Sugar Maple

State Flower: Wood Violet

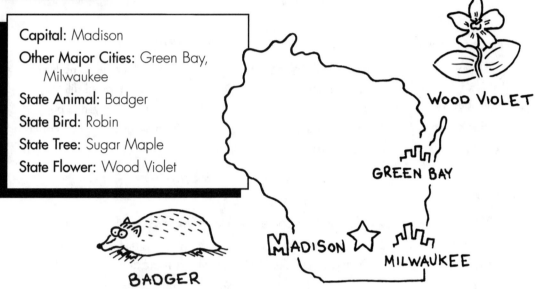

WOOD VIOLET

GREEN BAY

MADISON

MILWAUKEE

BADGER

This state's name comes from *wishkonsing*, an Ojibwa Indian word. This word may have had several meanings, including "place of the bearers." The first Europeans to explore Wisconsin were mostly French fur traders from Canada. Jean Nicolet was a well-known French explorer who was trying to find a passage to Asia. He was convinced that the Native Americans could help him find the passage, so he dressed in a silk robe from China in hopes that they would recognize it and point the way. However, when he landed at what is now Green Bay in 1634, the Winnebago tribe could offer only fur pelts and huge banquets. In 1672, France claimed Wisconsin, but the land passed to England when France lost the French and Indian War in 1763. After the United States won the Revolutionary War, what is now Wisconsin belonged to the United States. Wisconsin became the thirtieth state in 1848.

Wisconsin Foods

As you could guess from its nickname, Wisconsin is a leader in producing milk and milk products such as cheese and butter. Wisconsin also leads the country in growing peas, snap beans, and sweet corn.

•••• Wisconsin Cheddar Dill Puffs ••••

Time
20 minutes to prepare
plus
30 minutes to bake

Tools
cookie sheet

2-quart saucepan

wooden spoon

small bowl

fork

liquid measuring cup

oven mitts

spatula

wire rack

Makes
18 puffs

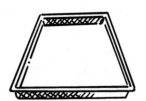

This is a great way to use Wisconsin cheese.

Ingredients

vegetable oil cooking spray

⅓ cup margarine

1 cup water

1 cup all-purpose flour

4 large eggs

½ cup shredded cheddar cheese

1 teaspoon dried dill

⅛ teaspoon cayenne pepper

2 tablespoons grated Parmesan cheese

Steps

1. Preheat the oven to 400°F.

2. Spray the cookie sheet with vegetable oil cooking spray.

3. Combine the margarine and water in the saucepan and bring to a boil. Boil until all the margarine is melted.

4. Add the flour to the pan all at once. Stir vigorously with the wooden spoon. Cook and stir on medium heat until the mixture forms a ball. Remove from the heat and cool for 10 minutes.

5. Break the eggs into the bowl and gently beat with a fork. Pour into the liquid measuring cup.

6. Add ¼ cup of the eggs to the flour mixture and beat well for 1 minute. Repeat with the rest of the egg, adding ¼ cup at a time and blending until smooth.

7. Beat in the shredded cheddar cheese, dill, and cayenne pepper.

8. Drop the dough by heaping tablespoons onto the cookie sheet. Space the pieces about ½-inch apart. Sprinkle each with Parmesan cheese.

9. Bake for about 30 minutes or until the puffs are golden brown and fluffy. Remove from the oven. With a spatula, put the puffs on the wire rack to cool for 10 minutes. Serve warm with margarine.

FUN FOOD FACTS

- Wisconsin farmers milk almost 2 million cows each day.
- The first malted milk was made in 1887 in Racine. A malted milk is made with milk, malted milk powder, and ice cream.
- The ice cream sundae originated in an ice cream parlor in Two Rivers in 1881. A customer requested some chocolate syrup, which was used to make ice cream sodas, on his ice cream. It soon became popular and the owner of the ice cream parlor started offering other toppings, such as nuts. When a neighboring town offered this fancy ice cream treat only on Sundays, it became known as a sundae. Why the spelling was changed is a mystery.

Fabulous Food Festival
Chocolate Festival
Burlington
(May)

PART 5

THE SOUTHWEST

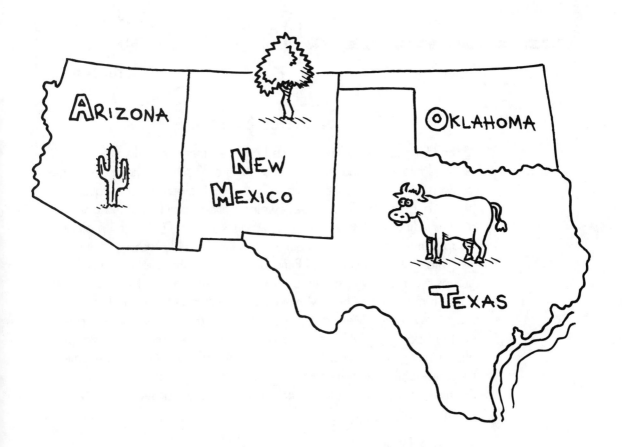

CHAPTER 36

RIZONA
The Grand Canyon State

Capital: Phoenix

Other Major Cities: Mesa, Tucson

State Bird: Cactus Wren

State Tree: Paloverde

State Flower: Saguaro Cactus Blossom

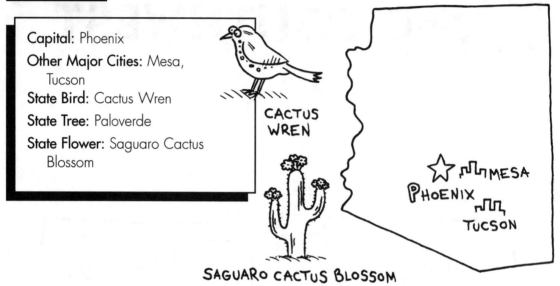

CACTUS WREN

SAGUARO CACTUS BLOSSOM

The Hohokam were an advanced Native American civilization who lived in the Arizona desert as long ago as 300 B.C. They built ditches to divert river water to their fields to grow their crops of corn, squash, beans, and cotton. They made jewelry, pottery, paintings, and even built a tall building to observe the stars. About A.D. 1450, the group all but disappeared, and no one is quite sure why. Possible reasons include war, drought, or famine. The Pima and several other Native American groups are probably descended from the Hohokams. In the late 1600s, Spanish missionaries from Mexico settled in Arizona. They called the area New Spain. Mexico took over the land after it became independent of Spain in 1821. The United States then took much of Arizona after winning a war with Mexico in 1848. In 1912 Arizona became the forty-eighth state. The name Arizona may have come from the Spanish pronunciation of *arizonac*, a Pima word that seems to have meant "small springs."

Arizona Foods

With irrigation and a long growing seasoning, farmers can grow citrus fruits, wheat, and lettuce. Farmers also raise livestock such as beef cattle.

Cheese Quesadilla with Vegetables

A quesadilla is made from two tortillas, traditionally filled with cheese and meat or vegetables, and baked. The basic recipe came to Arizona from Mexico.

Time
25 minutes

Tools
cookie sheet

medium bowl

cutting board

sharp knife

oven mitts

Makes
6 lunch servings

Ingredients

vegetable oil cooking spray

¾ cup shredded Monterey Jack cheese

¾ cup shredded cheddar cheese

1 teaspoon dried cilantro

1 teaspoon dried parsley

1 tomatillo (optional)

1 tomato

4 scallions

4 8-inch flour tortillas

¼ cup nonfat sour cream

4 tablespoons sliced black olives

Steps

1. Preheat the oven to 400°F. Spray the cookie sheet with vegetable oil cooking spray.

2. In the medium bowl, mix together the Monterey Jack cheese, cheddar cheese, cilantro, and parsley.

3. If using a tomatillo, remove its outer husk. Wash and dry the tomatillo, tomato, and scallions. On the cutting board, cut the tomatillo and tomato into small cubes. Slice the scallions into ¼-inch pieces. Set aside.

4. Place 2 tortillas on the cookie sheet. Cover each with the cheese mixture. Sprinkle with tomatillos, tomatoes, and scallions. Top with the second tortilla, pressing lightly to close.

5. Bake for 10 to 15 minutes or until the cheese is melted.

6. Remove the cookie sheet from the oven. Place 1 tablespoon sour cream on top of each quesadilla. Top with sliced olives. Cut each quesadilla into 6 wedges. Serve immediately.

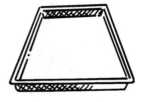

FUN FOOD FACTS

- Jicama, a popular vegetable grown in Arizona, has been called the Mexican potato. Like a potato, it has a brown skin and is a root vegetable. Unlike a potato, it has a crisp texture after being cooked and a slightly sweet taste. Jicama is commonly used in salads. It was brought to Arizona from Mexico.

- Tomatillos, which look like small green tomatoes with a thin, papery covering, are also grown in Arizona. They go back as far as the Aztecs. Tomatillos taste like lemons and herbs.

- Part of the prickly pear cactus is cooked in stews and used to makes jellies and candies.

Fabulous Food Festival

Arizona's Own Garlic Festival

Sedona
(June)

CHAPTER 37
NEW MEXICO
The Land of Enchantment

Capital: Santa Fe
Other Major Cities: Albuquerque,
    Las Cruces
State Bird: Roadrunner
State Tree: Piñon
State Flower: Yucca

ROADRUNNER   YUCCA

New Mexico was named for the country of Mexico, which in turn was named after Mexiti, an Aztec god. A group of Native Americans called the Anasazi lived over a thousand years ago in the Four Corners region where today New Mexico, Arizona, Colorado, and Utah meet. Like the Hohokam in Arizona, this group disappeared, and no one is quite sure why. Possible reasons include war, drought, or famine. The Pueblos, a group that includes several modern-day Native American tribes, are probably descended from the Anasazi. After 1539, New Mexico was controlled by Spain, which also ruled Mexico. In 1821, Mexico became independent and gained control of New Mexico. The United States took New Mexico from Mexico in 1848, and within two years the Territory of New Mexico, which included Arizona and parts of Colorado and Nebraska, was formed. In 1912, New Mexico became the forty-seventh state. Its nickname is the Land of Enchantment because of its scenic beauty and rich history.

···· Taco Soup ····

Time
60 minutes

Tools
knife

cutting board

large frying pan

wooden spoon

colander

large saucepan

Makes
8 servings

How would you like to slurp a taco? Here's a fun variation on a traditional New Mexico favorite.

Ingredients

1 small onion

vegetable oil cooking spray

1 pound lean ground beef, ground chicken, or ground turkey

1 16-ounce can tomato juice

1 16-ounce can kidney beans (do not drain)

1 8-ounce bottle chili sauce

1 17-ounce can whole kernel corn (do not drain)

2 teaspoons chili powder

8 tablespoons sour cream

Steps

1. Remove the outer skin of the onion. Using a knife on the cutting board, cut the onion in half and chop.

2. Spray the frying pan with the vegetable oil cooking spray. Heat the pan over low to medium heat.

3. Add the ground meat or poultry. With the wooden spoon, stir it around the pan as it cooks, to break up any large clumps. Cook the meat until it is browned.

4. Carefully pour the meat into a colander and allow the fat to drain.

5. Put the meat into the saucepan. Add the tomato juice, beans, chili sauce, corn, and chili powder.

6. Bring to a boil over high heat, then simmer on low for 45 minutes.

7. Serve in soup bowls. Put 1 tablespoon of sour cream on each serving.

New Mexico Foods

New Mexico is the leader in the country in producing chili peppers. Besides chili peppers, farmers also grow wheat, onions, and pecans. Many farmers also raise beef and dairy cattle.

FUN FOOD FACTS

- The country's oldest apple orchard can be found in a town called Manzano. *Manzano* means "apple tree" in Spanish. The orchard dates back to the 1600s.

- New Mexico is well known for its many different chili peppers. In fact, New Mexico grows over 200 different varieties! Much of the chili crop is dried and ground to make chili powder.

- The state tree of New Mexico is the piñon tree. From this tree come pine nuts. In the Southwest, pine nuts are used in salads, soups, stews, and some cakes.

Fabulous Food Festival
Feast Day in Taos Pueblo
Taos
(September)

CHAPTER 38

OKLAHOMA
The Sooner State

Capital: Oklahoma City

Other Major Cities: Lawton, Tulsa

State Bird: Scissor-tailed Flycatcher

State Tree: Redbud

State Flower: Mistletoe

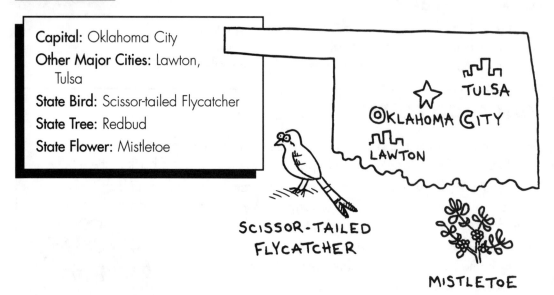

SCISSOR-TAILED FLYCATCHER

MISTLETOE

Before any European or American settlers came to Oklahoma, it was occupied by many groups of Native Americans, such as the Arapaho, Cheyenne, Comanche, Kiowa, and Osage. In 1803, only Native Americans lived in Oklahoma when it was bought by the United States from France as part of the Louisiana Purchase. Between 1820 and 1846, many Native American tribes were moved from eastern states to Oklahoma, most of them against their will. Some of the tribes that were relocated included the Cherokee, Chickasaw, Choctaw, Creek, and Seminole. The name Oklahoma comes from the Choctaw and means "home of the red people." Most of Oklahoma was considered Indian Territory until after the Civil War. In 1889, white settlers were allowed to settle on lands that had been leased to the Indians. Some tried to sneak onto the lands earlier than allowed, so they became known as "sooners." In 1907, Oklahoma became the forty-sixth state.

Oklahoma Foods

Beef and wheat are Oklahoma's two major cash crops. Farmers also grow peanuts and peaches.

Peanut Blondie Bars

Oklahoma produces both the peanuts and the wheat needed to make these delicious bar cookies.

Ingredients

vegetable oil cooking spray

½ cup smooth peanut butter

¼ cup margarine, softened

1 cup light brown sugar

2 large eggs

1½ teaspoons vanilla extract

⅔ cup all-purpose flour

1 cup chopped salted peanuts

Steps

1. Preheat the oven to 350°F. Spray the baking pan with vegetable oil cooking spray.

2. In the medium bowl with a wooden spoon, cream the peanut butter with the margarine until smooth.

3. Add the brown sugar gradually, beating until well blended.

4. Add the eggs one at a time and continue to stir. Add the vanilla extract.

5. Sift the flour into the small bowl. Slowly add flour to the peanut butter mixture. Fold in the peanuts.

6. Pour the batter into the prepared baking pan. Spread the batter evenly using a sandwich spreader.

7. Bake for 30 to 35 minutes. Remove the pan from the oven and cool for 15 minutes. Cut into 2-inch squares. Remove the blondies from the pan with the spatula and cool completely on the wire rack before serving.

Time

15 minutes to prepare
plus
30 to 35 minutes to bake

Tools

8-inch square baking pan

medium bowl

wooden spoon

small bowl

sifter

sandwich spreader

oven mitts

sharp knife

spatula

wire rack

Makes

16 squares

FUN FOOD FACTS

- An Oklahoman specialty is mung beans. They are grown for their sprouts, which are used in salads and many Asian dishes.
- Durum wheat, grown in Oklahoma, is used by large pasta manufacturing companies to make prepared pasta.

Fabulous Food Festival
Strawberry Festival
Stillwell
(May)

CHAPTER 39

TEXAS
The Lone Star State

Capital: Austin

Other Major Cities: Dallas, Houston

State Bird: Mockingbird

State Tree: Pecan

State Flower: Bluebonnet

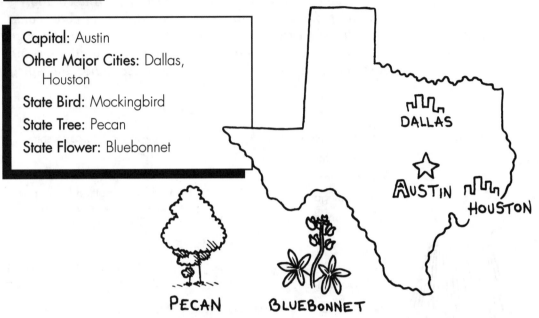

PECAN   BLUEBONNET

DALLAS

AUSTIN   HOUSTON

Texas got its name from a Native American word, *Tejas*, meaning "friends" or "allies." Tejas was the name of a group of tribes found in what is now Texas. Many tribes lived in Texas before Spanish explorers appeared in the early 1500s. The largest tribe was the Caddo in eastern Texas. Other groups included the Comanche on the prairies and the Arkokisa on the Gulf Coast. Spain first ruled Texas, then in 1821 it became a part of Mexico. In 1835, Texas fought for its independence from Mexico and won a year later. For about ten years Texas was an independent republic with a single star on its flag. That is how Texas became known as the Lone Star State. In 1845 Texas became the twenty-eighth state.

Texas Foods

Texas is the top state for raising beef cattle. Important crops include rice, peanuts, pecans, and citrus fruits. Commercial fishing boats on the Gulf of Mexico bring in shrimp, crabs, and fish.

Spicy Barbecue Sauce

Time
20 minutes

Tools
knife

cutting board

saucepan

Makes
1 ½ cups

Barbecues are a very important part of Texan cooking. Grilling foods over an open fire, hot stones, or coals, was a tradition carried on from the Native Americans. Brush this barbecue sauce on meat or poultry while it is grilling. Keep in mind that Texan barbecue sauce is hot and spicy!

Ingredients

1 medium onion

1 cup ketchup

½ cup water

¼ cup vinegar

2 tablespoons sugar

1 tablespoon Worcestershire sauce

¼ teaspoon ground cumin

3 to 4 drops bottled hot pepper sauce, or more as needed if you like it very hot

Steps

1. Cut the onion in half. Place the flat side down on the cutting board and chop enough to make ¼ cup.

2. Mix the onion, ketchup, water, vinegar, sugar, Worcestershire sauce, cumin, and hot pepper sauce in the saucepan.

3. Bring sauce to a boil. Reduce heat to low and simmer for 15 minutes.

4. Brush on meat or poultry during last 15 minutes of cooking.

FUN FOOD FACTS

- The Texas state food is chili, a spicy stew with ground beef and tomatoes. By the 1920s chili con carne was a Lone Star tradition. One of the basic ingredients of chili is hot chili peppers. Texans say their chili should be so hot that it makes them cry.

- Texas grows more blue corn than any other state. Blue corn is used to make tortillas and tortilla chips.

Fabulous Food Festival

Texas Citrus Festival

Mission (January/ February)

PART 6

THE ROCKY MOUNTAINS

CHAPTER 40

COLORADO
The Centennial State

Capital: Denver

Other Major Cities: Aurora, Colorado Springs

State Animal: Rocky Mountain Bighorn Sheep

State Bird: Lark Bunting

State Tree: Blue Spruce

State Flower: Rocky Mountain Columbine

ROCKY MOUNTAIN COLUMBINE

ROCKY MOUNTAIN BIGHORN SHEEP

Colorado means "colored red" in Spanish. This name was first given to the Colorado River because it flows through canyons with red stone, which gives the water a reddish tint. In the 1600s, early Spanish explorers found many groups of Native Americans living on the plains, including the Arapaho, Cheyenne, and Comanche. When the United States bought the Louisiana Territory in 1803, it included part of Colorado. The rest of Colorado became part of the United States after the Mexican War in 1848. Colorado had few settlers until 1858, when prospectors found gold near what is now Denver. Colorado became a territory in 1861 and was admitted as the thirty-eighth state in 1876. Its nickname, the Centennial State, comes from the fact that it became a state one hundred years after the United States declared its independence.

Colorado Foods

Colorado is a leader at raising beef cattle. Some ranchers also raise buffalo for their meat. Farmers grow crops such as wheat, potatoes, and apples.

···· Denver Sandwich ····

Chinese cooks working on the transcontinental railroad created the Denver sandwich, also known as a western sandwich or western omelet. It was actually Chinese Egg Fu Yung (an omelet) made with green peppers, onions, and chopped ham. It was placed between two pieces of bread and eaten as a sandwich.

Ingredients

4 eggs

2 tablespoons water

2 tablespoons margarine

½ cup chopped peppers

¼ cup chopped onions

¼ cup chopped mushrooms

¼ cup chopped ham

2 rolls or 4 slices of bread

Time
20 to 25 minutes

Tools
egg separator

medium bowl

large bowl

electric mixer

fork

rubber spatula

2 frying pans, 1 with an ovenproof handle

oven mitts

Makes
2 sandwiches

Steps

1. Remove the eggs from the refrigerator 45 minutes before starting this recipe.

2. Preheat the oven to 325°F.

3. Crack the eggs and use the egg separator to separate the whites from the yolks. Put the whites in the medium bowl and the yolks in the large bowl.

4. Beat the egg whites until stiff peaks form. The egg whites should be shiny and moist.

5. Beat the yolks with a fork and add the water.

6. Gently fold the egg whites into the yolk mixture using the rubber spatula.

7. Over low heat, melt 1 tablespoon of the margarine in the ovenproof frying pan.

8. Pour the eggs into the frying pan. Cook until the eggs are puffy, about 6 to 8 minutes.

9. Put the pan in the oven for 8 minutes or until a knife inserted in the center comes out clean.

10. While the omelet is baking, melt the other tablespoon of margarine in the other frying pan. Add the chopped peppers, onions, mushrooms and ham. Cook until tender, about 5 minutes.

11. Remove the pan from the oven. Use the spatula to loosen one side of the omelet.

12. Spoon the pepper mixture over half of the omelet. Fold the other half over to cover the pepper mixture.

13. Cut the omelet in half and place one half on each roll or between 2 slices of bread.

FUN FOOD FACTS

- Denver is known as the mile-high city. Its high elevation presents a challenge to cooks. Water boils at a lower temperature and baked goods tend to rise faster. Many recipes give directions for cooking at high altitudes.

- In pioneer days, "eating out" didn't mean going to a restaurant. It meant eating outside.

- The Denver Red Cake was first created at the Waldorf Astoria Hotel in New York City around 1900. A wealthy Colorado man supposedly paid $1,000 for the recipe and brought it back to Denver, where it became quite popular.

Fabulous Food Festival
Apple Fest
Cedaredge
(October)

CHAPTER 41

IDAHO
The Gem State

Capital: Boise

Other Major Cities: Idaho Falls, Pocatello

State Animal: Appaloosa

State Bird: Mountain Bluebird

State Tree: Western White Pine

State Flower: Syringa

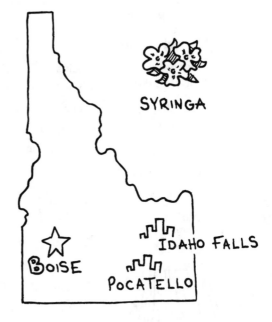

SYRINGA

APPALOOSA

BOISE

IDAHO FALLS

POCATELLO

When Meriwether Lewis and William Clark reached Idaho in 1805, they were the first white men to explore this area. They found many Native American groups, the largest of which were the Nez Perce and the Shoshone. Idaho was then part of the Oregon Territory, which was claimed by both the United States and England. In 1846 England withdrew its claims and this area became part of the United States. After gold was discovered in Idaho in 1860, thousands of prospectors came and many stayed. In 1860, the name Idaho was suggested for a new territory around Pike's Peak. The name supposedly meant "gem of the mountains," but it was rejected because it was not a real Indian word. The territory was named Colorado instead. The name Idaho, however, became popular and was used for a steamboat and a group of mines. In 1863, the name was suggested again, this time for the territory that includes present-day Idaho, Montana, and most of Wyoming. This time, it was accepted and the Idaho Territory was created. In 1890 Idaho became the forty-third state.

•••••• •••• Baked Sliced Potatoes •••• ••••••

Here's a wonderful way to serve Idaho spuds.

Time
15 minutes to prepare
plus
70 to 75 minutes to bake

Tools
3-quart baking dish

peeler

cutting board

knife

1-quart saucepan

oven mitts

Makes
6 servings

Ingredients

vegetable oil cooking spray
6 medium baking potatoes
⅔ cup margarine, melted
1 teaspoon kosher salt
1½ teaspoons dried thyme

1 teaspoon dried basil
1 teaspoon dried parsley
½ cup shredded cheddar cheese
2 tablespoons grated Parmesan cheese

Steps

1. Preheat the oven to 425°F. Spray the inside of the baking dish with vegetable oil cooking spray.

2. Wash and peel the potatoes.

3. On the cutting board, slice the potatoes into ¼-inch slices. Arrange in the baking dish.

4. Melt the margarine in the saucepan on low heat.

5. Drizzle the margarine over the potatoes. Sprinkle with the salt and herbs.

6. Bake the potatoes for 60 minutes.

7. Remove the baking dish from the oven with oven mitts. Leave the oven on.

8. Sprinkle the cheeses over the top of the potatoes, then put the dish back in the oven for 10 to 15 minutes or until the cheese is bubbly.

Idaho Foods

No state grows as many potatoes as Idaho. Farmers also grow dry beans, lentils, sugar beets, and wheat.

FUN FOOD FACTS

- French fries were first frozen by Jack Simplot in Idaho in the 1950s.
- Each year, Idaho potato growers produce about 100 million bags of potatoes that each weigh 100 pounds.
- The world's largest potato chip is in the Potato Museum in Blackfoot. The chip is 25 feet long and 14 feet wide.

Fabulous Food Festival
Idaho Spud Day
Shelley
(September)

WORLD'S LARGEST POTATO CHIP

CHAPTER 42
MONTANA
Big Sky Country

Capital: Helena

Other Major Cities: Billings, Great Falls

State Bird: Western Meadowlark

State Tree: Ponderosa Pine

State Flower: Bitterroot

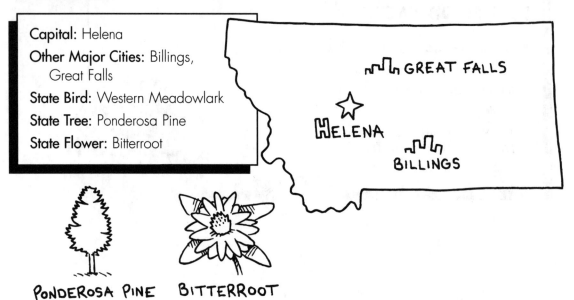

PONDEROSA PINE   BITTERROOT

The name Montana comes from the Spanish word for mountainous. Many groups of Native Americans, such as the Cheyenne, Crow, and Bannock, lived on Montana's plains and in its mountains before French trappers first visited the area in the middle 1700s. Most of Montana was part of the Louisiana Territory that France sold to the United States in 1803. In 1862 gold was found in Montana and many joined the goldrush. By 1864, the Montana Territory was created, and in 1889 Montana became the forty-first state. The western end of Montana is mountainous, but eastern Montana has vast plains. The wide view of the sky from these plains is what earned the state the nickname Big Sky Country.

Montana Foods

Montana is a leading cattle- and sheep-raising state. Farmers grow wheat, potatoes, and sweet black cherries.

···· Cheyenne Batter Bread ····

The Cheyenne used corn in many recipes, including breads made from cornmeal. When the Cheyenne were moved to reservations, they made variations to their traditional recipes, such as this one, that could be baked in ovens.

Ingredients

3 large eggs
4 tablespoons margarine
½ teaspoon salt

1 quart milk
2 cups yellow or white cornmeal
honey

Steps

1. Preheat the oven to 375°F.

2. Separate the egg whites from the yolks by cracking the eggs over an egg separator and a bowl. Make sure you get the yolk in the middle. The whites will drain out into the bowl. Put the yolks in a separate bowl.

3. Melt the margarine in the small saucepan.

4. Add the melted margarine and salt to the egg yolks. Beat well with a fork.

5. With the electric mixer, beat the egg whites until they stand in stiff peaks.

6. Over medium heat, bring milk to a boil in the large saucepan. Slowly stir in the cornmeal with the wooden spoon. Keep stirring until the mixture thickens. Remove from heat.

7. Add the egg yolk mixture to the cornmeal and stir well.

8. Using an over and under motion, gently fold the egg whites into the cornmeal mixture. Then pour the batter into the baking dish.

Time
45 minutes

Tools
egg separator
2 medium bowls
small saucepan
fork
electric mixer
large saucepan
wooden spoon
rubber spatula
2-quart baking dish

Makes
8 servings

9. Bake for 20 to 30 minutes or until the bread puffs up and is golden brown on top.

10. Slice and serve with honey.

FUN FOOD FACTS

- During hunting season, Montanans may have deer, moose, and elk meat to eat.
- There are four times as many beef cattle as people in Montana.

Fabulous Food
Festival
**Montana State
Chokecherry
Festival**
Lewistown
(September)

CHAPTER 43

NEVADA
The Sagebrush State

Capital: Carson City

Other Major Cities: Las Vegas, Reno

State Animal: Desert Bighorn Sheep

State Bird: Mountain Bluebird

State Trees: Bristlecone Pine, Single-leaf Pinyon

State Flower: Sagebrush

RENO

CARSON CITY

LAS VEGAS

SAGEBRUSH

MOUNTAIN BLUEBIRD

In Spanish, *nevada* means snow-covered. Indeed, Nevada has many mountains that are snow-covered year-round. During the early 1800s, Canadian fur traders entered Nevada and found Native American groups such as the Mohave, Shoshone, Paiute, and Washoe. Nevada was ruled by Spain and then by Mexico until 1848, when Mexico lost much of its northern territory to the United States in the Mexican War. Most of Nevada became part of the Utah Territory. In 1859, Nevada miners found one of the world's richest silver deposits, and called it the Comstock Lode after the miner Henry Comstock. This brought many prospectors to the area. In 1861, Nevada became a territory and three years later, during the Civil War, it became the thirty-sixth state. Nevada is nicknamed the Sagebrush State, as well as the Silver State. Sagebrush is a shrub that grows in the Nevada desert, which covers about one-fifth of the state.

Time
30 minutes

Tools
cutting board

knife

small bowl

wire whip

large pot

kitchen thermometer

tongs

2 cookie sheets

paper towels

Makes
6 servings

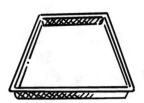

Nevada farmers grow lots of onions. Try this fun recipe to make your own onion rings.

Ingredients

2 large onions

1 cup pancake mix

¾ cup milk

⅛ teaspoon cayenne pepper

⅛ teaspoon salt

vegetable oil for deep frying

Steps

1. Preheat the oven to 300°F.

2. Remove the papery skin from the onion. Using a cutting board, cut the onion into ½-inch slices. Separate the slices into rings.

3. Put the pancake mix, milk, cayenne pepper, and salt in the small bowl, and whisk together until smooth.

4. Pour about 3 inches of oil into the large pot. Heat the oil to 375° F using a thermometer.

5. Dip the onion rings a few at a time into the batter. Then drop them in the oil and deep-fry until golden brown. Remove from the oil with the tongs and place on a cookie sheet covered with paper towels to drain.

6. Place the fried onion rings on the other cookie sheet and place it in the oven to keep them warm until serving. Serve immediately when all the onion rings are fried.

Nevada Foods

Nevada is the driest of all the states, but with the help of irrigation, some crops are grown, including potatoes, onions, and wheat. Beef cattle and sheep are raised.

FUN FOOD FACTS

- Two popular pioneer desserts were potato-caramel cake and saffron cake.
- Some Nevadans like to add lemon to their spaghetti sauce.

Fabulous Food Festival
The Best in the West Nugget Rib Cookoff
Sparks
(September)

CHAPTER 44
UTAH
The Beehive State

Capital: Salt Lake City

Other Major Cities: Ogden, Provo

State Bird: Seagull

State Tree: Blue Spruce

State Flower: Sego Lily

OGDEN

SALT LAKE CITY

PROVO

SEAGULL

SEGO LILY

Utah was named after the Ute Indians. Spanish priests from Mexico were the first to settle in this area and claimed the land for Spain in 1776. At that time, four major Native American groups were living there: the Ute, Gosiute, Paiute, and Shoshone. Spain controlled the land as part of Mexico until 1821, when Mexico became independent. In 1847, people of the Mormon religion were led to the Salt Lake Valley by Brigham Young to start a new life. About one year later, Mexico lost much of its northern territory to the United States in the Mexican War. In 1849 the Utah Territory was created. Many people traveled through Utah this time to get to California during the Gold Rush. In 1896, Utah became the forty-fifth state. When the Mormons settled in Utah, they called the region Deseret, a Mormon word meaning honeybee. The honeybee symbolizes hard work to the Mormons and this is why Utah is nicknamed the Beehive State.

···· Mallo-Mallo Fudge Squares ····

If you have a sweet tooth as big as Utah, try making this wonderful candy recipe with your family some night.

Ingredients

vegetable oil cooking spray

1 cup margarine (2 sticks)

4 cups sugar

12 fluid ounces evaporated milk

1¾ cups semisweet chocolate chips

1 10-ounce jar marshmallow crème

½ cup chopped pecans

1 teaspoon vanilla extract

Time
20 minute to cook
plus
3 hours to cool

Tools
12 x 9-inch baking pan

3-quart saucepan

wooden spoon

candy thermometer

sandwich spreader or table knife

paring knife

Makes
48 pieces

Steps

1. Spray the baking pan with vegetable oil cooking spray. Set aside.

2. Preheat the saucepan over medium heat for 1 minute.

3. Put the margarine in the saucepan. Stir with the wooden spoon until the margarine is melted.

4. Add the sugar and stir until it dissolves.

5. Add the evaporated milk and stir until well blended.

6. Clip a candy thermometer onto the side of the pan. Cook the mixture, stirring constantly, until the thermometer reaches 236°F.

7. Remove the pan from the heat and stir in the chocolate chips, marshmallow crème, pecans, and vanilla extract until well blended.

8. Pour the mixture into the sprayed pan and spread evenly with the sandwich spreader or table knife.

9. Use the paring knife to score the fudge into squares as if you were going to serve it. When you score fudge, you make a shallow notch or cut into it. Let the fudge cool in the pan at room temperature for about 3 hours. Once it is cool, you can cut it and remove from the pan.

Utah Foods

Utah farmers mostly raise livestock such as beef cattle, dairy cattle, and turkeys. Because of the dry climate, irrigation has to be used to grow wheat, potatoes, apples, and peaches.

FUN FOOD FACTS

- The residents of Utah eat about twice as much candy per person than people in any other state. They also rank near the top in ice cream consumption.

- The Mormon church encourages families to spend one evening together in an activity each week. Candymaking is a popular activity on these nights.

Fabulous Food Festival
Strawberry Days Festival
Pleasant Grove
(June)

CHAPTER 45

WYOMING
The Cowboy State

Capital: Cheyenne

Other Major Cities: Casper, Laramie

State Animal: Bison

State Bird: Meadowlark

State Tree: Cottonwood

State Flower: Indian Paintbrush

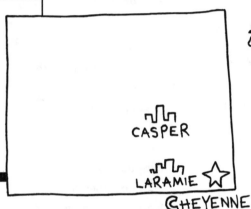

BISON

INDIAN PAINTBRUSH

The name Wyoming comes from a Delaware Indian word meaning "at the big, large plains." The Delaware were an eastern tribe who used the name for a valley in Pennsylvania. It was an Ohio congressman who suggested the name for the Wyoming Territory. French fur trappers from Canada may have been the first to enter Wyoming in the mid-1700s. At that time, many Native American groups lived there. They included tribes such as the Bannock, Blackfeet, Cheyenne, Sioux, and Ute. The United States bought most of this area from France in 1803 as part of the Louisiana Purchase. Many pioneers heading west went through Wyoming. The California, Mormon, and Oregon Trails all took Wyoming's South Pass through the Rocky Mountains. Wyoming became a U.S. territory in 1868, and in 1890 it became the forty-fourth state. Wyoming is known as the Cowboy State because of all its ranches. It is also called the Equality State because it was the first state to grant women the right to vote and hold public office.

Wyoming Foods

Most of Wyoming land is used to raise beef cattle, dairy cattle, sheep, and other livestock. Important crops include dry beans, wheat, and potatoes.

Time
45 minutes

Tools
cookie sheet

cutting board

knife

3-quart saucepan

wooden spoon

wire whip

rolling pin

3-inch biscuit cutter

small bowl

pastry brush

oven mitts

ladle

12 3-inch disposable
tartlet tins
or
pie pans

Makes
12 pot pies

Beef pot pie makes a hearty evening meal for people who work on ranches all day.

Ingredients

vegetable oil cooking spray

4 scallions

1 green pepper

½ cup margarine

½ cup flour

1 teaspoon garlic salt

1 teaspoon dried thyme

1 teaspoon dried oregano

3 cups canned beef broth

1 cup light cream

1 package frozen mixed vegetables, cooked according to package directions

1 teaspoon dried parsley

3 cups cubed leftover cooked beef, such as steak or roast beef

1 package frozen puff pastry, thawed

1 egg

1 teaspoon water

Steps

1. Preheat the oven to 400°F. Spray the cookie sheet with vegetable oil cooking spray.

2. Using the cutting board, cut the root ends and green tips off the scallions. Slice into ¼-inch rings.

3. Cut the green pepper in half. With the knife, remove the seeds and the ribs. Cut in half again. Cut each piece into long strips, then chop into small pieces.

4. Preheat the saucepan over medium heat for 2 minutes. Melt the margarine. Add the scallions and green peppers. Cook the vegetables until tender, about 3 to 4 minutes, stirring occasionally with the wooden spoon.

5. Slowly blend in the flour, stirring constantly.

6. Add the garlic salt, thyme, and oregano and continue to stir.

7. Slowly whisk the beef broth and light cream into the mixture. Bring to a boil. Lower the heat to medium and cook, stirring constantly until the sauce thickens.

8. Stir in the cooked vegetables, parsley, and beef cubes. Remove from the heat.

9. On a lightly floured surface, roll out one sheet of the pastry with the rolling pin. Use the biscuit cutter to cut out 12 round disks. Place the disks on the cookie sheet.

10. In the small bowl, mix the egg and the water together. Using a pastry brush, brush the pastry disks with the egg mixture.

11. Bake for 15 to 20 minutes or until the pastry is puffy and lightly golden brown. Remove from the oven with oven mitts.

12. To assemble the pies, reheat the filling. Ladle about ¾ cup of the beef mixture into each foil tin. Place the pastry disks on top and serve.

FUN FOOD FACTS

- A variety of Asian vegetables, such as snowpeas, are grown in Wyoming and there are many Chinese restaurants. Chinese people first came to Wyoming to work on the railroads.

Fabulous Food
Festival
**Chugwater Chili
Cookoff**
Chugwater
(June)

PART 7

THE PACIFIC STATES

CHAPTER 46

ALASKA
The Last Frontier

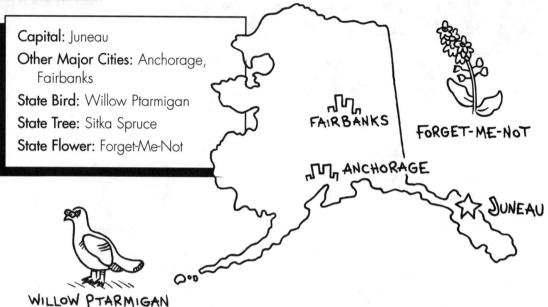

Capital: Juneau

Other Major Cities: Anchorage, Fairbanks

State Bird: Willow Ptarmigan

State Tree: Sitka Spruce

State Flower: Forget-Me-Not

FAIRBANKS

FORGET-ME-NOT

ANCHORAGE

JUNEAU

WILLOW PTARMIGAN

The word *Alaska* comes from the Aleut word *alyeska*, meaning "great land." There were three major native groups living in Alaska: the Inuit (or Eskimos), the Aleuts of the southwestern peninsula and the islands, and the Tlingit and Athabascan Indians of the southeast and central regions. Because of Alaska's location on the northwest tip of the North American continent close to Russia, Russia controlled parts of the area from about 1800. Russian fur traders were very active there. In 1867 the United States bought Alaska from Russia. Some Americans made fun of the purchase and called it "Seward's Folly" after Secretary of State William H. Seward, who promoted the purchase. But Alaska had vast natural resources such as fish, copper, and coal, and in 1897 gold was discovered in the Yukon Territory, a part of Canada just across the Alaska-Canada border. Many prospectors made the trip through Alaska to the Yukon. In 1900 gold was discovered in Alaska and prospectors crowded into Nome. By 1912, Alaska became a territory. In 1959 Alaska was admitted as the forty-ninth state. It is nicknamed the Last Frontier because much of Alaska is not settled.

Baked Salmon

Alaska is the biggest producer of salmon in the world. Salmon was one of the most important foods of many native Alaskans before the arrival of explorers and settlers. Five species of salmon are found in Alaska's 2,000 rivers. Try this easy recipe to taste the mild, yet distinctive, flavor of salmon.

Time
25 minutes

Tools
shallow baking pan

small frying pan

Makes
4 servings

Ingredients

vegetable oil cooking spray

1 pound skinless salmon fillets, fresh or frozen, ½ inch thick (thaw frozen fish overnight in refrigerator)

2 tablespoons butter or margarine

1 tablespoon lemon juice

dash salt

dash pepper

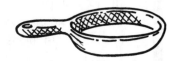

Steps

1. Preheat oven to 400°F.

2. Cut the fish into 4 serving-size pieces if necessary.

3. Spray the baking pan with vegetable oil cooking spray. Place the fillets in a single layer in the baking pan.

4. In the frying pan, melt the butter or margarine over low heat. Once it is melted, remove it from heat and add the lemon juice, salt, and pepper.

5. Pour the butter or margarine mixture over the fillets.

6. Bake for 12 to 18 minutes or until the fish flesh separates easily when tested with a fork.

Alaska Foods

Alaska is the leader in the United States in seafood production. Important fish include salmon, pollock, cod, halibut, and ocean perch. Although little Alaskan land is farmland, some crops, beef cattle, and poultry are raised. Milk is the most important agricultural product.

FUN FOOD FACTS

- The halibut caught off of Alaska weigh between 100 and 300 pounds.
- The main farming region is the Matanuska Valley. The vegetables grown there are huge. A fifty-pound cabbage or a strawberry as large as your fist are not unusual. The long daylight hours and cool temperatures help plants grow and store starch and sugar. The flavors of these big vegetables are also more intense than those of regular varieties.
- Snow ice is an Alaskan dessert made with evaporated milk, sugar, vanilla, and fresh snow.

Fabulous Food Festival
Kodiak Crab Festival
Kodiak
(May)

CHAPTER 47

CALIFORNIA
The Golden State

Capital: Sacramento

Other Major Cities: Los Angeles, San Diego

State Bird: California Valley Quail

State Tree: California Redwood

State Flower: Golden Poppy

CALIFORNIA VALLEY QUAIL

SACRAMENTO

LOS ANGELES

SAN DIEGO

CALIFORNIA REDWOOD

Spanish explorers who sailed along its coast in the 1500s named California after a treasure island in a Spanish tale. In the 1760s and 1770s, Spanish people came from Mexico to establish forts and missions at what are now San Diego and San Francisco. The Spaniards found many Native American groups living there, including the Hupa, Maidu, Quechan, and Pomo. Spain was forced to give California to Mexico when Mexico won its independence from Spain in 1821, but Mexico only loosely controlled the area at any point. Mexico gave California to the United States after losing the Mexican War in 1848. In that same year, gold was discovered, and settlers flocked to the region. These gold hunters became known as '49ers. In 1850, California became the thirty-first state. California may have acquired the nickname the Golden State for several reasons: its fields of golden poppies (the state flower), its golden-brown hills, and the Gold Rush.

··· Classic Caesar Salad ···

Time
15 minutes

Tools
paper towels

large salad bowl

cutting board

knife

colander

Makes
8 servings

Caesar salad was first made by an Italian restaurant owner named Caesar Cardini in Tijuana, Mexico, in 1924. The recipe was a big hit with Hollywood stars who traveled to Tijuana. It became very popular in Los Angeles and eventually across the United States.

Ingredients

1 large head romaine lettuce

1 head iceberg lettuce

1 cup bottled Caesar salad dressing

1 cup grated Parmesan cheese

1 cup croutons

Steps

1. Wash the romaine lettuce leaves and lay on paper towels to dry. Tear the leaves into bite-sized pieces and place in the salad bowl.

2. Remove the outer leaves from the iceberg lettuce. On a cutting board, cut the lettuce in half. Cut out the heart in the center and discard. Lay the lettuce halves flat side down on the cutting board and slice into ¼-inch strips. Place in a colander to wash. Dry thoroughly. Add to the salad bowl and toss.

3. Add the salad dressing to the salad bowl. Toss the salad greens with the dressing until well coated.

4. Arrange the salad on serving plates. Top each serving with 2 tablespoons of Parmesan cheese and 2 tablespoons of croutons. Serve immediately.

California Foods

California's more than 75,000 farms bring in more income than farms in any other state. Because of the excellent climate and good farmland, California farmers grow a wide variety of fruits, nuts, and vegetables, especially grapes, almonds, lettuce, and tomatoes. Dairy and beef cattle are also raised.

FUN FOOD FACTS

- California supplies more than half of the produce (fresh fruits and vegetables) in the United States.

- California is the number one producer of lemons. They were introduced in the 1700s by the Franciscan Fathers, a religious group that had come from Mexico to establish missions in California.

- California has food festivals for a wide variety of foods: oranges, garlic, raisins, pumpkin, asparagus, artichokes, mustard, and tamales, to name just a few!

Fabulous Food
Festival
Stockton Asparagus Festival
Stockton
(April)

CHAPTER 48

AWAII The Aloha State

Capital: Honolulu
Other Major Cities: Kailua, Pearl City
State Bird: Nene (Hawaiian Goose)
State Tree: Kukui (Candlenut)
State Flower: Yellow Hibiscus

PEARL CITY
KAILUA
HONOLULU

YELLOW HIBISCUS

NENE (HAWAIIAN GOOSE)

Hawaii is a chain of islands in the North Pacific Ocean, 2,400 miles from the west coast of the United States mainland. The name Hawaii probably came from the word *Hawaiki*, the legendary name of the Polynesian homeland to the west. Hawaii's first inhabitants were Polynesians (Pacific Islanders) from Tahiti and other South Pacific islands who arrived in canoes over 1,500 years ago. In 1778, British captain James Cook discovered the islands and named them the Sandwich Islands after the Earl of Sandwich. Many other European traders followed. The native population welcomed their visitors, but unfortunately many were wiped out by European diseases. In 1900, Hawaii became a territory of the United States after having asked several times to be annexed. However, it was not until 1959 that Hawaii was admitted as the fiftieth state. It is called the Aloha State because *aloha* was a nineteenth-century Hawaiian word for love that was used as both a greeting and farewell.

Hawaii Foods

Hawaii is well known for producing pineapples, sugar cane (used to make sugar), macadamia nuts, and papayas. The macadamia nut grows on tall evergreen trees. Hawaiian farms also produce milk and eggs. The fishing industry is big business in Hawaii and the most important fish are swordfish and tuna.

Pineapple Chicken Kabobs

This recipe uses pineapple to make a delicious supper on a stick.

Ingredients

water
2 medium onions
2 green peppers
1 zucchini
12 cherry tomatoes
1½ pounds boneless chicken cutlets

2 cups pineapple chunks, drained
⅓ cup soy sauce
3 tablespoons honey
1 tablespoon vegetable oil
1 teaspoon Worcestershire sauce
vegetable oil cooking spray

Time
15 minutes to prepare
plus
10 minutes to cook

Tools
bamboo skewers
cutting board
knife
skewers
small bowl
wire whip
broiler pan
oven mitts

Makes
6 kabobs

Steps

1. Soak the bamboo skewers for 45 minutes in warm water. Remove and dry.

2. Remove the outer papery skin of the onion. Using the cutting board, cut each onion in half. Lay each onion half flat on the cutting board and cut in half again.

3. Wash and dry the green peppers, zucchini, and tomatoes.

4. Cut each green pepper in half. Remove and discard the seeds and ribs from the inside of the pepper. Cut each pepper half into four wedges.

5. Slice the zucchini into ¼-inch slices. Cut each slice in half.

6. Cut the chicken into 2-inch pieces.

7. To assemble the kabobs, place 1 chicken piece, 1 onion piece, 1 pepper wedge, 1 zucchini slice, 1 tomato, and 1 pineapple chunk on a skewer. Repeat this pattern on the same skewer.

8. Fill the other 5 skewers.

9. In the bowl, whisk together the soy sauce, honey, oil, and Worcestershire sauce.

10. Spray the broiler pan with vegetable oil cooking spray. Preheat the broiler.

11. Place the kabobs on the pan and brush them with the soy sauce mixture.

12. Place the kabobs about 6 inches from the heating element or flame and broil them for 5 to 6 minutes. Watch carefully.

13. Using oven mitts, slide the broiler pan out. Turn the kabobs over and brush again with the soy sauce mixture.

14. Broil 3 to 4 minutes more. Watch carefully.

15. Using oven mitts, remove the pan and place the skewers on plates.

FUN FOOD FACTS

- Thanks to the Hawaiians, we enjoy luaus, or feasts, usually held outdoors. The early luaus were held to thank the gods. Later, luaus were held for special events, such as weddings or birthdays. The centerpiece of a luau is a pig wrapped in leaves and roasted in a pit. Other luau foods include poi (the cooked stem of the taro plant made into a paste), limu (seaweed), teriyaki (meat or seafood broiled with a sauce), and fresh fruits such as pineapple, banana, and papaya.

- Over 600,000 tons of pineapples are harvested in Hawaii each year. James Dole came from Boston in 1899 and developed pineapple growing into a major industry.

- Hawaii is the only state with a climate hot and moist enough to grow coffee.

Fabulous Food Festival
Macadamia Nut Harvest Festival
Hawaii (October)

CHAPTER 49

OREGON
The Beaver State

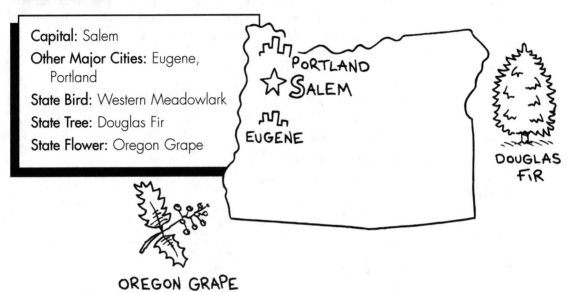

Capital: Salem

Other Major Cities: Eugene, Portland

State Bird: Western Meadowlark

State Tree: Douglas Fir

State Flower: Oregon Grape

PORTLAND
SALEM
EUGENE

DOUGLAS FIR

OREGON GRAPE

Oregon probably got its name from the French word *ouragan*, meaning "hurricane." The name was first used for the major river that runs through the state, then for the area around the river. Native American groups such as the Tillamook, Paiute, and Bannock were living in the area when Europeans first arrived. While explorers had sailed along Oregon's coast and up some rivers since 1543, Meriwether Lewis and William Clark were probably the first to explore by land. In 1818, the United States and Britain agreed that both would occupy Oregon. In 1843, increasing numbers of American settlers started to come to Oregon using the Oregon Trail. By 1846, Britain had given up its control of what are now Washington and Oregon. Two years later the Oregon Territory was established. In 1859, Oregon became the thirty-third state. Oregon is nicknamed the Beaver State because of all the beaver skins it produced during the years of the fur trade. Oregon is also called the Pacific Wonderland because of all its natural wonders, such as the Cascade Mountains and the Hells Canyon on the Snake River.

Cranberry Cookie Bars

Time
15 minutes to prepare
plus
30 minutes to bake

Tools
9 x 13 x 2-inch
baking pan

cutting board

knife

medium bowl

large bowl

wooden spoon

oven mitts

wire rack

Makes
20 bars

Cranberries are grown in bogs or marshes in the coastal regions of Oregon. Cranberries blossom in late June or early July, and the berry harvest begins right after Labor Day.

Ingredients

2 teaspoons shortening

1 cup fresh cranberries

1 ½ cups sifted flour

1 teaspoon baking powder

½ teaspoon salt

½ cup margarine (1 stick)

1 cup sugar

½ cup brown sugar, packed

2 large eggs

1 teaspoon vanilla extract

Steps

1. Preheat the oven to 350°F. Grease the baking pan with the shortening.

2. Wash and dry the cranberries. Chop them on the cutting board.

3. In the medium bowl, combine the flour, baking powder, and salt.

4. In the large bowl, cream the margarine with the sugar and brown sugar by pushing the mixture against the bowl with the back of the wooden spoon. Add the eggs one at a time, beating after each addition.

5. Stir in the vanilla extract.

6. Mix the flour mixture into the sugar and egg mixture.

7. Fold in the cranberries with a gentle over-and-under motion.

8. Spread the batter in the pan and bake for 30 minutes. Cool on a wire rack for 20 minutes.

9. When cool, cut into bars.

Oregon Foods

Oregon grows a wide variety of crops, in part because of its variations in climate and geography. Oregon leads the nation in winter pears, blackberries, boysenberries, and hazelnuts. Other products include potatoes, carrots, watermelons, cranberries, cheeses, and fish (especially salmon, halibut, ling cod, and shellfish).

FUN FOOD FACTS

- Almost all the hazelnuts produced in this country are grown in Oregon. A Frenchman from an area in France called the Loire Valley, which is similar in climate to Oregon, brought fifty young hazelnut seedlings with him.

- Over twenty different kinds of clams can be found along the coast. One clam, called the geoduck clam, digs into the sand. You'll know if you've found its home because it will squirt water up through the sand into the air when you step on the sand directly over it.

- One of the most famous gourmets in the United states, James Beard, was born in Portland. He always encouraged using fresh ingredients such as fruits and vegetables from his home state.

Fabulous Food
Festival
Pear Blossom Festival
Medford
(April)

CHAPTER 50

WASHINGTON
The Evergreen State

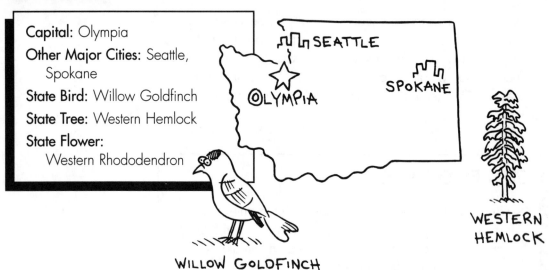

Capital: Olympia

Other Major Cities: Seattle,
   Spokane

State Bird: Willow Goldfinch

State Tree: Western Hemlock

State Flower:
   Western Rhododendron

OLYMPIA

SEATTLE

SPOKANE

WILLOW GOLDFINCH

WESTERN
HEMLOCK

Washington was named after the first president of the United States, George Washington. In 1775, when Spanish explorers landed near Point Grenville, the area was inhabited by many groups of Native Americans such as the Spokane, Walla Walla, Chinook, and Quinault. During the early 1800s, British and American fur traders set up trading posts in Washington. In 1818, the United States and Britain agreed that both would occupy Washington, but by 1846 Britain agreed to let the United States keep the land. Two years later the Oregon Territory, which included Washington, was established. In 1853, the Washington Territory was carved out of the Oregon Territory, and in 1889, Washington became the forty-second state. Washington is nicknamed the Evergreen State because it has so many pine trees, fir trees, and other evergreen trees.

Washington Foods

Washington is first in the nation in growing apples. Farmers also grow lots of wheat, potatoes, asparagus, peas, and carrots. Fishing boats bring in salmon, trout, and halibut.

•••••••• •••• **Baked Apples** •••• ••••••••

Apples are Washington state's number one agricultural product. Each year 10 to 12 billion apples are harvested. The Red Delicious is the most popular variety, contributing to over half of the state's production.

Ingredients

vegetable oil cooking spray

4 Red Delicious or Golden Delicious apples

¼ cup brown sugar

½ teaspoon cinnamon

¼ teaspoon ground nutmeg

⅛ teaspoon ground cloves

1 teaspoon margarine

¼ cup golden raisins

1 cup water

Steps

1. Preheat the oven to 375°F. Spray the baking pan with vegetable oil cooking spray.

2. Wash the apples and pat dry.

3. On a cutting board, remove the cores from the apples using an apple corer. Using a knife, slice ¼-inch off the bottom of the apples.

4. Place the apples in the baking pan so they stand upright.

5. In the small bowl, mix together the brown sugar, cinnamon, nutmeg, and cloves.

6. Place the margarine in the microwave-safe dish and melt on full power for about 30 to 60 seconds. Mix the margarine with the brown sugar mixture. Fold in the raisins.

7. Fill the center of each apple with the brown sugar mixture. Pour 1 cup of water around the apples.

8. Bake for 50 to 60 minutes until the apples are soft. Using the cooking spoon, spoon the liquid from the bottom of the pan over the apples to keep them moist before serving.

Time
15 minutes to prepare
plus
50 to 60 minutes to bake

Tools
9-inch square baking pan

cutting board

apple corer

knife

small bowl

microwave-safe dish

large cooking spoon

Makes
4 baked apples

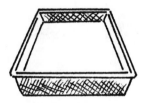

FUN FOOD FACTS

- Of all the apples grown in Washington, 70 percent are Red Delicious and 25 percent are Golden Delicious. Other apples include Granny Smiths, Romes, and Newtons.

- Washington is well-known for a very sweet onion called the Walla Walla. It is grown in the Walla Walla Valley.

- Prospectors searching for gold in the 1800s were called "sourdoughs" because they carried sourdough starter with them to make sourdough bread.

Fabulous Food Festival
Apple Blossom Festival
Wenatchee
(April/May)

INDEX

Alabama, 52–54
Alaska, 162–64
Alligator meat, 60
Appetizers
    crab cakes (Maryland), 40–41
    taco soup (New Mexico), 132
Apple Blossom Festival, 176
Apple Fest, 144
Apple orchard, oldest, 133
Apples
    Golden Delicious, 86–87, 176
    Red Delicious, 98, 175, 176
Apples, recipes with
    baked apples (Washington), 175
    Golden Delicious apple pie (West Virginia),
        86–87
    raspberry and apple cobbler (New
        Hampshire), 26–27
Appleseed, Johnny, 119
Appliances, safety rules, 12
Arizona, 128–30
Arizona's Own Garlic Festival, 130
Arkansas, 55–57

Badlands, 122
Baked apples (Washington), 175
Baked salmon (Alaska), 163
Baked sliced potatoes (Idaho), 146
Baking pan, 4
Banana berry pancakes with real maple syrup
    (Vermont), 32–33
Bananas, imports, 38
Bananas, recipes with
    banana berry pancakes with real maple
        syrup (Vermont), 26–27
    peanutty peanut butter and banana bread
        (Georgia), 62
Barbecue (North Carolina), 74–75

Barbecue sauce (Texas), 138
Beans
    Boston baked beans (Massachusetts), 23
    Cincinnati chili over pasta (Ohio), 118–19
Bean Soup Festival, 50
Beard, James, 173
Beaten biscuits, 41
Beating, 8
Beef, recipes with
    Cincinnati chili over pasta (Ohio), 118–19
    grilled Swiss cheeseburger with sliced mush-
        rooms (Kansas), 100
    Kentucky burgoo, 65–66
    rancher's beef pot pies (Wyoming), 158–59
    Reuben Sandwich (Nebraska), 112
    Swedish meatballs (Minnesota), 106
    taco soup (New Mexico), 132
Beef pot pies (Wyoming), 158–59
Ben & Jerry's ice cream, 33
Berries, recipes with
    banana berry pancakes with real maple
        syrup (Vermont), 26–27
    blueberry cornbread (Maine), 20
    cranberry cookie bars (Oregon), 172
    raspberry and apple cobbler (New
        Hampshire), 26–27
The Best in the West Nugget Rib Cookoff, 153
Biscuit cutter, 4
Biscuits, sweet potato (Alabama), 53–54
Black Hawk, Chief, 96
Black Walnut Festival, 87
Black walnut quickbread (Missouri), 109
Blueberry cornbread (Maine), 20
Blue corn, 139
Bluegrass, 64
Boiling, 9
Boone, Daniel, 64
Borden Company, 24

Boston baked beans (Massachusetts), 23
Bread pudding (Indiana), 94
Breads
   black walnut quickbread (Missouri), 109
   blueberry cornbread (Maine), 20
   Cheyenne batter bread (Montana), 149–50
   New Orleans pain perdu (Louisiana), 68
   peanutty peanut butter and banana bread
      (Georgia), 62
   sweet potato biscuits (Alabama), 53–54
Breakfast foods
   banana berry pancakes with real maple
      syrup (Vermont), 32–33
   cornmeal mush with molasses (South
      Dakota), 121
   Denver sandwich (Colorado), 143–44
Burgoo, Kentucky, 65–66
Butter or margarine, equivalents, 8

Cabot Creamery, 33
Caesar salad (California), 166
Cajuns, 69
Cakes
   Election day cake (Connecticut), 17–18
California, 165–67
Calvert, Cecil, 39
Campbell Soup Company, 44
Candy consumption, 156
Cane sugar syrup, 107
Cardini, Caesar, 166
Carteret, Sir George, 42
Carver, George Washington, 54
Catfish, 72
Cereal Festival, 104
Chapman, John Jr. (Johnny Appleseed), 119
Charles I (King of England), 39, 73, 76
Charles II (King of England), 28, 42, 76, 82
Cheddar dill puffs (Wisconsin), 124
Cheese, recipes with
   baked sliced potatoes (Idaho), 146
   cheese quesadilla with vegetables (Arizona),
      129
   deep dish pizza (Illinois), 91

grilled Swiss cheeseburger with sliced mush-
      rooms (Kansas), 100
   macaroni and cheese (North Dakota), 115
   Reuben Sandwich (Nebraska), 112
   Wisconsin cheddar dill puffs, 124
Cheeseburgers
   first U.S. cheeseburger, 66
   grilled Swiss cheeseburger with sliced mush-
      rooms (Kansas), 100
Cheesecake, 47
Cheese manufacturers, 33
Cheese quesadilla with vegetables (Arizona),
   129
Cherry Festival, 119
Cherry sauce, recipes with
   ice cream with cherry sauce in a tortilla shell
      (Michigan), 103
   Virginia ham with cherry sauce (Virginia), 83
Chewing gum, first invented, 21
Cheyenne batter bread (Montana), 149–50
Chicken, recipes with
   Kentucky burgoo, 65–66
   pineapple chicken kabobs (Hawaii), 169–70
Chicken industry, 38
Chicken kabobs, pineapple (Hawaii),
   169–70
Chili, 139
Chili over pasta, Cincinnati (Ohio), 118–19
Chocolate
   mallo-mallo fudge squares (Utah), 155
   Mississippi mud pie, 71
   rice pudding (Arkansas), 55–56
Chocolate Festival, 125
Chocolate rice pudding (Arkansas), 56–57
Chopping, 7
Chowder, defined, 18
Chugwater Chili Cookoff, 159
Cincinnati chili over pasta (Ohio), 118–19
Clambakes, 30
Clam Festival, 21
Clark, George Rogers, 90
Clark, William, 145, 171
Classic Caesar salad (California), 166

Classic gingerbread squares (Delaware), 37
Cleaning up, safety rules, 13
Coca-Cola, 63
Coffee Burger, 113
Coffee milkshakes (Rhode Island), 29
Colander, 4
Colorado, 142–44
Comstock, Henry, 151
ConAgra, 113
Connecticut, 16–18
Cook, James, 168
Cookie bars, cranberry (Oregon), 172
Cookie sheet, 4
Cornbread
  blueberry (Maine), 20
  Cheyenne batter bread (Montana), 149–50
Corn dogs (Iowa), 97–98
Corned beef, recipes with
  Reuben Sandwich (Nebraska), 112
Cornmeal mush with molasses (South Dakota), 121
Corn Palace (South Dakota), 122
Crab cakes (Maryland), 40–41
Cracking and separating eggs, 9–10
Cranberry cookie bars (Oregon), 172
Cranberry Harvest Festival, 24
Crawfish, 69
Creaming, 8
Cream of Wheat, 116
Creoles, 69
Cup, equivalents, 8
Cutting, commonly used terms, 7
Cutting board, 4

Declaration of Independence, 48
Deep dish pizza (Illinois), 91
Delaware, 36–38
De La Warr, Lord, 36
Denver Red Cake, 144
Denver sandwich (Colorado), 143–44
Desserts
  baked apples (Washington), 175
  black walnut quickbread (Missouri), 109

bread pudding (Indiana), 94
chocolate rice pudding (Arkansas), 55–56
classic gingerbread squares (Delaware), 37
coffee milkshakes (Rhode Island), 29
cranberry cookie bars (Oregon), 172
Election day cake (Connecticut), 17–18
Golden Delicious apple pie (West Virginia), 86–87
ice cream with cherry sauce in a tortilla shell (Michigan), 103
key lime pie (Florida), 59
mallo-mallo fudge squares (Utah), 155
Mississippi mud pie, 71
New Orleans pain perdu (Louisiana), 68
peach roll (South Carolina), 77
peanut blondie bars (Oklahoma), 135
raspberry and apple cobbler (New Hampshire), 26–27
Dicing, 7
Dole, James, 170
Dorrance, John, 44
Durum wheat, 115, 136

East Tennessee Strawberry Festival, 81
Egg Festival, 95
Eggs
  cracking and separating, 9–10
  Denver sandwich (Colorado), 143–44
Egg separator, 4
Election day cake (Connecticut), 17–18
Electric blender, 4
Electric mixer, 4
Elizabeth I (Queen of England), 82
Elsie the Cow, 24
Equivalents, 8

Feast Day in Taos Pueblo (food festival), 133
Festival of Gingerbread, 95
Fish
  baked salmon (Alaska), 163
  crab cakes (Maryland), 40–41
Fishing, commercial, 29
Florida, 58–60

Florida Citrus Festival, 60
Folding, 8
Food festivals
  Apple Blossom Festival, 176
  Apple Fest, 144
  Arizona's Own Garlic Festival, 130
  Bean Soup Festival, 50
  The Best in the West Nugget Rib Cookoff, 153
  Black Walnut Festival, 87
  Cereal Festival, 104
  Cherry Festival, 119
  Chocolate Festival, 125
  Chugwater Chili Cookoff, 159
  Clam Festival, 21
  Cranberry Harvest Festival, 24
  East Tennessee Strawberry Festival, 81
  Egg Festival, 95
  Feast Day in Taos Pueblo, 133
  Festival of Gingerbread, 95
  Florida Citrus Festival, 60
  French Food Festival, 69
  Grape Festival, 92
  Ham & Yam Festival, 75
  Hope Watermelon Festival, 57
  Idaho Spud Day, 147
  International Bar-B-Q Festival, 66
  International Pancake Race, 101
  International Quahog Festival, 30
  Kodiak Crab Festival, 164
  Lobster Weekend, 18
  Macadamia Nut Harvest Festival, 170
  Montana State Chokecherry Festival, 150
  Mount Washington Valley Chocolate Festival, 27
  National Hard Crab Derby and Fair, 41
  National Shrimp Festival, 54
  New Jersey Seafood Festival, 44
  Oyster Festival, 47, 78, 84
  Ozark Ham and Turkey Festival, 110
  Pear Blossom Festival, 173
  Popcorn Festival, 95
  Potato Bowl, 116
  Rockwood's Victorian Ice Cream Festival, 38
  Schmeckfest, 122
  Seafood Festival, 72
  Stockton Asparagus Festival, 167
  Strawberry Days Festival, 98, 156
  Strawberry Festival, 136
  Taste of Minnesota Food Festival, 107
  Texas Citrus Festival, 139
  Vermont Maple Festival, 33
  Vidalia Onion Festival, 63
  Wayne Chicken Show, 113
French Food Festival, 69
French fries, 147
Frito-Lay Inc., 81
Frogmore Stew, 78
Frogs' legs, 60
Fruits, recipes with
  baked apples (Washington), 175
  banana berry pancakes with real maple syrup (Vermont), 32–33
  blueberry cornbread (Maine), 20
  cranberry cookie bars (Oregon), 172
  Golden Delicious apple pie (West Virginia), 86–87
  ice cream with cherry sauce in a tortilla shell (Michigan), 103
  key lime pie (Florida), 59
  peach roll (South Carolina), 77
  peanutty peanut butter and banana bread (Georgia), 62
  pineapple chicken kabobs (Hawaii), 169–70
  raspberry and apple cobbler (New Hampshire), 26–27
  Virginia ham with cherry sauce (Virginia), 83
  Waldorf salad (New York), 46
Frying pan, 6
  world's largest, 75

Gallon, equivalents, 8
George II (King of England), 61
Georgia, 61–63
German potato salad (Tennessee), 80–81
Gingerbread Festival, 95
Gingerbread squares (Delaware), 37

Golden Delicious apple pie (West Virginia), 86–87
Golden Delicious apples, 86–87, 176
Gold Rush, 145, 148, 154, 162, 165, 176
Good Humor Ice Cream, 119
Grape Festival, 92
Grater, 5
Grating, 7
Green, Robert M., 50
Green Giant, 107
Grilled Swiss cheeseburger with sliced mushrooms (Kansas), 100
Ground beef, recipes with
    Cincinnati chili over pasta (Ohio), 118–19
    grilled Swiss cheeseburger with sliced mushrooms (Kansas), 100
    Swedish meatballs (Minnesota), 106
    taco soup (New Mexico), 132

Halibut, 164
Ham, Virginia, with cherry sauce (Virginia), 83
Ham and pork, recipes with
    Denver sandwich (Colorado), 143–44
    North Carolina BBQ, 74–75
    Virginia ham with cherry sauce (Virginia), 83
Hamburgers
    Coffee Burger, 113
    first hamburger, 18
    first U.S. cheeseburger, 66
    grilled Swiss cheeseburger with sliced mushrooms (Kansas), 100
Hams, 81, 83
Ham & Yam Festival, 75
Harvey House (Topeka, Kansas), 101
Hatch, Sir Robert, 73
Hawaii, 168–70
Hershey, Milton, 50
Hope Watermelon Festival, 57
Horseradish, 92
Hot dogs, 110
    corn dogs (Iowa), 97–98
Hush puppies, 72
Hustead, Ted and Dorothy, 122

Ice cream, 33
    cones, 110
    consumption, 156
    sodas, 50
    stick, on, 119
    sundaes, 125
Ice cream with cherry sauce in a tortilla shell (Michigan), 103
Idaho, 145–47
Idaho Spud Day (food festival), 147
Illinois, 90–92
Indiana, 93–95
Indians. *See* Native Americans
International Bar-B-Q Festival, 66
International Pancake Race (food festival), 101
International Quahog Festival, 30
Iowa, 96–98
Italian submarine sandwiches (New Jersey), 43

James (Duke of York), 45
James I (King of England), 82
Jefferson, Thomas, 84, 120
Jicama, 130
Johnnycakes, 30

Kaelin's Restaurant (Louisville), 66
Kansas, 99–101
Kay, Reuben, 112
Kellogg, John Harvey, 104
Kentucky, 64–66
Kentucky burgoo, 65–66
Kentucky Fried Chicken, 66
Ketchup, tomato, 84
Key lime pie (Florida), 59
Knives
    described, 5
    safety rules, 13
Kodiak Crab Festival, 164
Kraft, 92
Kroc, Ray, 92

La Salle, 67, 70, 96
Lay, Herman, 81

Layer cake pans, 5
Lay's Potato Chips, 81
Lemons, 167
Lewis, Meriwether and Clark, William,
   145, 171
Lincoln, Abraham, 107, 120
Lindy's restaurant (New York), 47
Lobster, early settlers and, 21
Lobster Weekend (food festival), 18
Louisiana, 67–69
Louis Rich, 92
Louis XIV (King of England), 67, 70, 99

Macadamia Nut Harvest Festival, 170
Macaroni and cheese (North Dakota), 115
Main dishes
   baked salmon (Alaska), 163
   Cincinnati chili over pasta (Ohio), 118–19
   corn dogs (Iowa), 97–98
   crab cakes (Maryland), 40–41
   deep dish pizza (Illinois), 91
   Denver sandwich (Colorado), 143–44
   grilled Swiss cheeseburger with sliced mush-
      rooms (Kansas), 100
   Italian submarine sandwiches (New Jersey), 43
   Kentucky burgoo, 65–66
   macaroni and cheese (North Dakota), 115
   North Carolina BBQ, 74–75
   pineapple chicken kabobs (Hawaii), 169–70
   rancher's beef pot pies (Wyoming), 158–59
   Reuben Sandwich (Nebraska), 112
   Swedish meatballs (Minnesota), 106
   taco soup (New Mexico), 132
   Virginia ham with cherry sauce (Virginia), 83
Maine, 19–21
Mallo-mallo fudge squares (Utah), 155
Maple syrup
   facts on, 31, 32, 107
   recipe with, 26–27
Marshmallows
   mallo-mallo fudge squares (Utah), 155
Maryland, 39–41
Maryland baked crab cakes, 40–41

Mason, John, 25
Massachusetts, 22–24
McDonald's restaurants, 92
McIlhenny family, 69
Measuring, 8
Measuring cups, 5
Measuring spoons, 5
Meat dishes
   Cincinnati chili over pasta (Ohio), 118–19
   Denver sandwich (Colorado), 143–44
   grilled Swiss cheeseburger with sliced mush-
      rooms (Kansas), 100
   Kentucky burgoo, 65–66
   North Carolina BBQ, 74–75
   pineapple chicken kabobs (Hawaii), 169–70
   rancher's beef pot pies (Wyoming), 158–59
   Reuben Sandwich (Nebraska), 112
   Swedish meatballs (Minnesota), 106
   taco soup (New Mexico), 132
   Virginia ham with cherry sauce (Virginia), 83
Mennonites, 101
Mexican dishes
   cheese quesadilla with vegetables (Arizona),
      129
   Cincinnati chili over pasta (Ohio), 118–19
   taco soup (New Mexico), 132
Michigan, 102–4
Microwave dish, 5
Microwave oven, 12
Middle Atlantic
   Delaware, 36–38
   Maryland, 39–41
   New Jersey, 42–44
   New York, 45–47
   Pennsylvania, 48–50
Midwest
   Illinois, 90–92
   Indiana, 93–95
   Iowa, 96–98
   Kansas, 99–101
   Michigan, 102–4
   Minnesota, 105–7
   Missouri, 108–10

Nebraska, 111–13
North Dakota, 114–16
Ohio, 117–19
South Dakota, 120–22
Wisconsin, 123–25
Milkshakes, coffee (Rhode Island), 29
Mincing, 7
Minnesota, 105–7
Mississippi, 70–72
Mississippi mud pie, 71
Missouri, 108–10
Mixing, 8
Mixing bowls, 5
Money crop, first, 78
Montana, 148–50
Montana State Chokecherry Festival, 150
Montpelier biscuits, 33
Mormons, 154, 156
Mount Washington Valley Chocolate
    Festival, 27
Mud pie, Mississippi, 71
Muffin tins, 5
Mung beans, 136
Mush, cornmeal with molasses (South
    Dakota), 121

National Hard Crab Derby and Fair (food
    festival), 41
National Shrimp Festival, 54
Native American dish
    Cheyenne batter bread (Montana), 149–50
Native Americans
    chewing gum, 21
    corn, use by Cheyenne, 149
    Delaware Bay, 36
    early civilization, 128, 131
    rice harvesting, 107
    sweet potatoes, farming, 53
    tribe names, 16
Nebraska, 111–13
Nebraska Consolidated Mills, 113
Nestlé Company, 24
Nevada, 151–53

New England
    Connecticut, 16–18
    Maine, 19–21
    Massachusetts, 22–24
    New Hampshire, 25–27
    Rhode Island, 28–30
    Vermont, 31–33
New Hampshire, 25–27
New Jersey, 42–44
New Jersey Seafood Festival, 44
New Mexico, 131–33
New Orleans pain perdu (Louisiana), 68
New York, 45–47
Nicolet, Jean, 123
North Carolina, 73–75
North Carolina BBQ, 74–75
North Dakota, 114–16
Nuts, recipes with
    black walnut quickbread (Missouri), 109
    peanut blondie bars (Oklahoma), 135
    peanutty peanut butter and banana bread
        (Georgia), 62

Oatmeal, 119
Oglethorpe, General James, 61
Ohio, 117–19
Oklahoma, 134–36
Onion rings (Nevada), 152
Orange trees, 60
Oregon, 171–73
Oscar Mayer, 92
Oven, safety rules, 11–12
Oyster Festival, 47, 78, 84
Ozark Ham and Turkey Festival, 110

Pacific states
    Alaska, 162–64
    California, 165–67
    Hawaii, 168–70
    Oregon, 171–73
    Washington, 174–76
Pain perdu (Louisiana), 68
Palm hearts, 60

Pancakes
  banana berry pancakes with real maple
    syrup (Vermont), 32–33
  syrup, 107
Pan-fry, 9
Pans, described, 6
Paring knife, 5
Pasta dishes
  Cincinnati chili over pasta (Ohio), 118–19
  macaroni and cheese (North Dakota), 115
Pasteur, Louis, 44
Pasties, 104
Pastry blender, 6
Peach roll (South Carolina), 77
Peanut blondie bars (Oklahoma), 135
Peanut butter, 110
Peanuts, 63
  research on, 54
Peanuts, recipes with
  peanut blondie bars (Oklahoma), 135
  peanutty peanut butter and banana bread
    (Georgia), 62
Peanutty peanut butter and banana bread
    (Georgia), 62
Pear Blossom Festival, 173
Pecans, harvesting, 110
Peeler, 5
Penn, William, 48
Pennsylvania, 48–50
Pennsylvania Dutch, 49, 50
Pepsi-Cola, 63, 75
Perky, Henry, 47
Philadelphia soft pretzels (Pennsylvania),
    49–50
Pies
  Golden Delicious apple pie (West Virginia),
    86–87
  key lime pie (Florida), 59
  Mississippi mud pie, 71
  rancher's beef pot pies (Wyoming), 158–59
Piggly Wiggly supermarket, 81
Pillsbury, Charles, 107
Pillsbury (company), 107

Pineapple chicken kabobs (Hawaii), 169–70
Pine nuts, 133
Pink tomatoes, 57
Pizza, deep dish (Illinois), 91
Pizza Hut restaurant, 101
Ponce de Leon, Juan, 58
Popcorn, 95
Popcorn Festival, 95
Post, C. W., 104
Potato Bowl (food festival), 116
Potato chips, 81, 147
Potatoes
  baked sliced potatoes (Idaho), 146
  farming of, 21, 27
  French fries, 147
  German potato salad (Tennessee), 80–81
  potato chips, 81, 147
  sweet potato biscuits (Alabama), 53–54
Potato salad, German (Tennessee), 80–81
Pot pies, beef (Wyoming), 158–59
Pretzels, soft (Pennsylvania), 49–50
Prickly pear cactus, 130
Puddings
  bread pudding (Indiana), 94
  chocolate rice pudding (Arkansas), 55–56

Quahogs, 30
Quart, equivalents, 8
Quesadilla, cheese (Arizona), 129
Quickbread, black walnut (Missouri), 109

Raleigh, Sir Walter, 73, 82
Rancher's beef pot pies (Wyoming), 158–59
Raspberry and apple cobbler (New
    Hampshire), 26–27
Red Delicious apples, 98, 175, 176
Redenbacher, Orville, 95
Red Flannel Hash, 27
Reuben Sandwich (Nebraska), 112
Rhode Island, 28–30
Rhode Island Red, 30
Rice, crops, 78, 107
Rice pudding, chocolate (Arkansas), 55–56

Rockwood's Victorian Ice Cream Festival, 38
Rocky Mountains
    Colorado, 142–44
    Idaho, 145–47
    Montana, 148–50
    Nevada, 151–53
    Utah, 154–56
    Wyoming, 157–59
Rolling pin, 6
Roosevelt, Theodore, 120
Rubber spatula, 6
Russian fur trade, 162

Safety rules, 11–13
Salads
    classic Caesar salad (California), 166
    Waldorf salad (New York), 46
Salmon, baked (Alaska), 163
Sanders, "Colonel" Harland, 66
Sandwiches
    Denver sandwich (Colorado), 143–44
    grilled Swiss cheeseburger with sliced mush-
        rooms (Kansas), 100
    Italian submarine sandwiches
        (New Jersey), 43
    North Carolina BBQ, 74–75
    Reuben Sandwich (Nebraska), 112
Sandwich spreader, 5
Saucepan, 6
Sauces
    ice cream with cherry sauce in a tortilla shell
        (Michigan), 103
    spicy barbecue sauce (Texas), 138
    Virginia ham with cherry sauce (Virginia), 83
Sauté, 9
Schmeckfest (food festival), 122
Seafood Festival, 72
Separating eggs, 9–10
Seward, William H., 162
"Seward's Folly," 162
Shoofly pie, 50
Shredded Wheat Company, 47
Shredding, 7

Side dishes
    baked sliced potatoes (Idaho), 146
    Boston baked beans (Massachusetts), 23
    German potato salad (Tennessee), 80–81
    onion rings (Nevada), 152
Simmer, 9
Sioux Sundries, 113
Skills, cooking, 7–10
Slicing, 7
Snacks
    coffee milkshakes (Rhode Island), 29
    peanutty peanut butter and banana bread
        (Georgia), 62
    Philadelphia soft pretzels (Pennsylvania),
        49–50
    Wisconsin cheddar dill puffs, 124
Snow ice, 164
Soups
    canning of, 44
    taco soup (New Mexico), 132
Sourdough, 176
South
    Alabama, 52–54
    Arkansas, 55–57
    Florida, 58–60
    Georgia, 61–63
    Kentucky, 64–66
    Louisiana, 67–69
    Mississippi, 70–72
    North Carolina, 73–75
    South Carolina, 76–78
    Tennessee, 79–81
    Virginia, 82–84
    West Virginia, 85–87
South Carolina, 76–78
South Dakota, 120–22
Southwest
    Arizona, 128–30
    New Mexico, 131–33
    Oklahoma, 134–36
    Texas, 137–39
Spatula, 6
Spicy barbecue sauce (Texas), 138

Spoons, described, 6
Stark, General John, 25
Stark Brothers Nursery (Iowa), 98
Steam, 9
Steel, Cecil, 38
Stews
  Kentucky burgoo, 65–66
Stockton Asparagus Festival, 167
Stove, safety rules, 11–12
Stovetop cooking, 9
Strawberry Days Festival, 98, 156
Strawberry Festival, 136
Submarine sandwiches, Italian (New
  Jersey), 43
Supermarket, world's first, 81
Swedish meatballs (Minnesota), 106
Sweet potato biscuits (Alabama), 53–54
Swift Premium, 92
Syrup
  cane sugar, 107
  maple, 26–27, 31, 32, 107

Tabasco Sauce, 69
Table knife, 5
Tablespoon, equivalents, 8
Taco soup (New Mexico), 132
Taste of Minnesota Food Festival, 107
Tea plantation, first, 78
Teaspoon, 6
  equivalents, 8
Tennessee, 79–81
Texas, 137–39
Texas Citrus Festival, 139
Toll House Cookies, 24
Tomatillos, 130
Tonti, Henry de, 55
Tools for cooking, described, 4–6
Tortilla shell, ice cream with cherry sauce in
  (Michigan), 103
Towle, Patrick J., 107
Tube pan, 6

Utah, 154–56

Varsity restaurant (Atlanta), 63
Vegetarian dishes
  cheese quesadilla with vegetables (Arizona),
    129
  onion rings (Nevada), 152
Vermont, 31–33
Vermont Maple Festival, 33
Victoria (Queen of England), 84
Vidalia Onion Festival, 63
Virginia, 82–84
Virginia ham with cherry sauce
  (Virginia), 83
The Virginia Housewife, 84

Waldorf Astoria (New York), 46, 144
Waldorf salad (New York), 46
Walla Walla onions, 176
Wall Drug (South Dakota), 122
Washington, 174–76
Washington, George, 45, 120, 174
Watermelons, 57
Wayne Chicken Show (food festival), 113
West, Thomas, 36
West Virginia, 85–87
Whipping, 8
Whisking, 8
White, Governor John, 73
Wilder, Laura Ingalls, 121
Williams, Roger, 28
Wire rack, 6
Wire whip, 6
Wisconsin, 123–25
Wisconsin cheddar dill puffs, 124
Wooden spoon, 6
Wyoming, 157–59

Yogurt, first, 24

MAR 2005